—— MIND MATTERS ——

Does God Exist?

——————— MIND MATTERS ———————

Series Editor: Judith Hughes

In the same series

—————— MIND MATTERS ——————

does God exist?

MARK CORNER

THE BRISTOL PRESS

To Sarah Caden

A CIP catalogue record for this book is available from the British Library

ISBN 1 85399 164 3

First published in 1991 by:

Bristol Classical Press
226 North St
Bedminster
Bristol BS3 1JD

© Mark Corner 1991

The Bristol Press is an imprint of Bristol Classical Press

Printed in Great Britain by
Billing & Sons Ltd, Worcester

contents

foreword

'A philosophical problem has the form *I don't know my way about,*' said Wittgenstein. These problems are not the ones where we need information, but those where we are lost for lack of adequate signposts and landmarks. Finding our way — making sense out of the current confusion and becoming able to map things both for ourselves and for others — is doing successful philosophy. This is not quite what the lady meant who told me when I was seven that I ought to have more philosophy, because philosophy was eating your cabbage and not making a fuss about it. But that lady *was* right to suggest that there were some useful skills here.

Philosophising then, is not just a form of highbrow chess for postgraduate students; it is becoming conscious of the shape of our lives, and anybody may need to do it. Our culture contains an ancient tradition which is rich in helpful ways of doing so, and in Europe they study that tradition at school. Here, that study is at present being squeezed out even from university courses. But that cannot stop us doing it if we want to. This series contains excellent guide-books for people who do want to, guide-books which are clear, but which are not superficial surveys. They are themselves pieces of real philosophy, directed at specific problems which are likely to concern all of us. Read them.

MARY MIDGLEY

preface

In the original preface to the Mind Matter' series, I wrote;
Philosophers are very good at talking to one another. Some
of them are also good at talking with other people... ' Mind
Matters is not 'Philosophy Made Easy' but rather Philosophy
Made Intelligible and the authors in this series have been
chosen for more than their philosophical knowledge. Some
of them are also experts in other fields such as medicine,
computing or biology.

The aim of the series was to open up philosophy to a wide
general public by producing books which were clear, intelligible, meaningful and original and written in a lively and
engaging manner. Pleasingly, the books have proved popular
with a wide general readership and also are now used on a
variety of university and college courses for lawyers, health
workers, artists, teachers and computer scientists as well as
philosophers. These latest volumes continue the attempt to
communicate philosophical ideas to all those who, for a great
variety of reasons, find themselves questioning the foundations of their beliefs.

Each book begins with a perplexing question that we may
ask ourselves without, perhaps, realising that we are 'philosophising': Do computers have minds? Can a pile bricks be a
work of art? Should we hold pathological killers responsible
for their crimes? Such questions are considered and new
questions raised with frequent reference to the views of major
philosophers. The authors go further than this, however. It is
not their intention to produce a potted history of philosophical
ideas. They also make their own contributions to the subject,

suggesting different avenues of thought to explore. The result is a collection of original writings on a wide range of topics produced for all those who find philosophy as fascinating and compelling as they do.

It is tempting for philosophers and theologians brought up in the Western rationalist tradition to interpret the question 'Does God exist?' as meaning either 'Can God exist?' or 'Must God exist?' These interpretations invite answers which have more to do with logic and semantics than with faith, and none of them are beyond criticism. The usual alternative is to regard belief in God's existence as a pure leap of faith, beyond reason or evidence. Mark Corner considers both these views and then reclaims the question from both the logician and the mystic. If there is a God, he argues, it is at least consistent with the fact that we should experience an intellectual uncertainty about it. The silence of God in the world cannot be taken as a sign of his non-existence: rather it is entirely compatible with his existence.

Mark Corner does not set out to convert or to comfort, but in his honest approach to matters of the deepest significance to us all, he shows a way to think which may well help some of us along the road.

introduction

There is a tendency for books on God to be sure that they have the answers, whether in terms of His existence or His non-existence. Cocksure believers compete with unbelievers who 'grew out of all that sort of thing at the age of ten'. My hope is that this book might at least make the question 'Does God exist?' meaningful, interesting and worthy of further consideration.

This is not the first book with the title *Does God Exist?* Many people will recall the encyclopaedic work by Hans Küng which has the same title in translation. Some may remember the work by Professor A.E. Taylor written much longer ago. In length and approach, this book is closer to Taylor than to Küng. It cannot begin to discuss all the major writers and opinions on the subject. It intends to help people to become interested in the question and to read more, rather than claiming to provide a definitive answer.

This book attempts to recognise that this question cannot be asked as if it is of interest only to the Judaeo-Christian. Although I have to admit that my main training is in the Judaeo-Christian tradition, I have tried to bring other traditions into consideration in a significant way. Hopefully my approach is not one that fails to recognise the multi-faith context within which 'Does God exist?' is asked in the Western world today.

The book is divided into six main chapters. The first two set out to examine what sort of answer we can expect to the question that forms the title of the book. That may seem a peculiar thing to say — just a straight 'yes' or 'no' will do! But the point is a serious one. The philosophy of religion gives a great deal of consideration to so-called 'proofs' of God's existence. The assumption might appear to be that if God existed then it ought to be possible to demonstrate that existence with mathematical certainty. This assumption is put to the test in these two chapters, suggesting that it is not inconsistent to suppose that a God might exist who did not wish us to know, or at least to be sure, that He existed. Uncertainty as to whether or not God exists may therefore be consistent with belief in God, and should not necessarily be dismissed as 'agnosticism'. The inability to 'prove' God's existence, in the sense of demonstrating it in such a way that its denial would be a contradiction, does not necessarily entail the collapse of theism. It could even be argued that certain forms of theism would collapse if such a proof *were* to be available. For instance if one wanted to argue that God does not coerce belief, might not a corollary of this argument be that there could be no certainty God existed?

Having argued that the evidence for God's existence does not need to be as great as some atheists (and theists) believe it to be, I will attempt in the rest of the book to examine it in detail. I adopt a tradition that distinguishes between the 'physical' attributes of the Deity, such as 'eternity', 'infinity' and 'omnipotence', and the 'moral' attributes such as 'wisdom', 'love and 'justice'. The former I consider in the third and fourth chapters, the latter I look at in the fifth and sixth. In order to go along with the theists, we need to know more than that there is a God: we need to know that this God has a good purpose. Many atheists find the goodness of God at least as difficult to accept as His existence. I try to do justice to this question by devoting a third of the book to what is traditionally termed 'theodicy' — the problem of evil.

In the course of the book I use 'He' to describe God because this is familiar practice. However, I would like to say at the outset that the pronoun 'She' could have been used with equal validity. Few world religions, and none of the ones that we consider in this book, define God as a person, whether male or female; but most employ both male and female symbols in their imagery of God. The authorities, whether clerical or academic, that have maintained these religions have on the whole been men, so the female imagery which exists in the sacred literature of these traditions is often neglected in their theology.

In this book I try to advance the view that God's relation to the world can only be understood in terms of divine self-limitation, a restraint that allows humanity 'room to breathe'. It is arguable that a history of male images for God — as king, emperor, judge, and even father — has obscured the way in which God respects the independence and autonomy of creation. That point might have been grasped more easily if female images of God, for instance as mother, nurse or midwife, had been accorded more prominence.

In his famous *Letters and Papers from Prison*, the German theologian Dietrich Bonhoeffer explored from a Nazi prison cell the idea that God, as Christians conceive Him, limits Himself in order to give human beings freedom to accept or reject Him. That self-limitation may even mean that God embraces weakness — as reflected in the powerful Christian imagery of God on a cross. To Bonhoeffer it meant that God was teaching us to live *etsi Deus non daretur* — as if there were no God. Thus the process of secularisation was no threat to Him; he saw it as a means by which humanity 'came of age' and, by learning to interpret reality without the need to assume the existence of God, achieved a divinely-willed maturity.

There are many problems with Bonhoeffer's view, not least the moral problems. The sort of 'maturity' that comes through God's unwillingness to intervene in the world might be thought to be gained at too high a cost by those who, like Bonhoeffer himself, had to come to terms with an historical process which threw up instances of evil like Nazism. Slowly but surely, day by day, month by month, thousands and eventually millions of Jewish men, women and children went to their deaths, whilst the rest of Europe remained in ignorance or looked on carelessly. German and Polish railway workers changed the points to allow the trains to roll into the death camps, and British civil servants suppressed documents that might have ensured the railway lines were bombed. But above all the silence was God's. No parting of the Red Sea for these Jews; just a slow and excruciating drowning. For many of them, crucifixion might have been thought a mild alternative to their own suffering.

Nevertheless, it is Bonhoeffer's vision which more than any other has informed this small book. If there is a God, would He create the sort of ambiguous and confusing world we happen to live in? Even that is an impossible question to answer; but my main hope, as I have said, is to encourage further thought and reading from those with a better understanding than can be expressed here.

1: the meaning of theism

theists, atheists and the chance of an argument

In the first chapter I attempt to set out some of the different forms of theism and atheism. By doing so, I hope to show that the dialogue between believers and non-believers in God can proceed only on the basis of certain common assumptions. Some theists and atheists can talk to one another, and some cannot. It therefore becomes necessary to outline what must be agreed upon between both sides if the argument is to be taken further.

To define the different forms of theism and atheism is no easy task, and it requires from the start a degree of modesty and admission that we cannot hope to cover everything! 'Metaphysics' has been defined as the attempt by a blind man in a dark room to find a black hat which isn't there. For the rest of this book an attempt is being made to explore some metaphysical questions — so perhaps we are entitled to stumble.

That said, some progress, stumbling or not, must be attempted. The many forms of atheism can usefully be divided into two categories. The first category is made up of those who can make no sense whatever of any God-talk. It is all mumbo-jumbo. The question of whether God exists is irrelevant because the word 'God' has no meaning. This group would answer the question: 'Does God exist?' by saying: 'I don't know what you're talking about'. I will label them 'no meaning' atheists.

Secondly, there are those with a clear idea of what 'God' means. I will label them 'meaning' atheists. That is to say, they know what it would be like for God to exist, but as a matter of fact they don't think that one does.

'No meaning' atheists tend to talk rather as A.J. Ayer talks in *Language, Truth and Logic,* as if there is no possibility of a Deity existing because there is no possibility of making sense of the word 'God':

> ....if 'god' is a metaphysical term, then it cannot even be probable that a god exists. For to say that 'God exists' is to make a metaphysical utterance which cannot be either true or false. And by the same criterion, no sentence which purports to describe the nature of a transcendent god can possess any literal significance.

Ayer's position appears to be making the rules so that the theist cannot win. In effect he says: you can't be a theist unless you use metaphysical terms. Metaphysical terms are meaningless. Therefore anything you say about God is meaningless.

Some people might imagine that the three positions of theist, agnostic and atheist could be defined as follows: the theist knows there is a God; the agnostic doesn't know whether there's a God or not; the atheist knows there is not a God. If this were true, there would at least be common ground between the three, in that they all agreed what was meant by the word 'God'. The argument could then turn to whether there was one. But Ayer represents what is probably more often the position of the atheist, namely that it simply makes no sense to talk of God. Asking whether God exists has no more meaning than a grunt or a belch.

We see here the way in which battle is often joined between theist and atheist. The theist will want to argue that you cannot talk of God in the way that you talk of other things. This may require him or her to use what might be called 'metaphysical' terms. But he or she will then have to demonstrate that it is possible to make sense when using such terms. The argument about God thereby becomes an argument about language. Rather than arguing about whether God exists, the theist and the atheist find themselves arguing about whether metaphysical terms have meaning.

If we now turn from atheists to theists, we find that the forms of theism can be categorised in a similar manner. For instance, there is the 'no meaning' theist. An example of this position can be found in the writings of Karl Barth, probably the most famous Christian theologian of the twentieth century.

Barth thought that if we knew what we meant by the word 'God', then God must exist. He expounded his theory in a work on Anselm entitled *Fides Quaerens Intellectum* (Faith Seeking Understanding). Barth was deeply impressed by Anselm's so-called 'Ontological Argument' for the existence of God — this argument will be looked at in more detail later — but he interpreted it in a particular way. He thought that precisely because it was impossible for the human mind to construct an idea of God from its inherent mental resources, such an idea could only be given to it by revelation — in other words directly implanted by God Himself. Because there could be no idea of God in the mind without God putting it there, an idea of God was impossible without God's existence. Barth therefore concluded that it was correct to argue that if we could define God then God must exist. It was as if the idea of God in the mind was like a shadow thrown on a wall. It could not be there unless the object reflected in this way existed.

Barth and Ayer have elements in common. Both insist that language about God admits of no connection with 'ordinary' language, and that in terms of 'ordinary' language it is meaningless. But where one concludes from this that theistic terms cannot be understood, the other concludes that they are the language of 'faith', directly given to the believer by God. They agree that theological discourse does not make sense in the terms of ordinary language, but whereas for one this effectively consigns theology to the dustbin, for the other it gives it the same sort of status as speaking in tongues. It represents a direct divine revelation that delivers a capacity for understanding beyond the parameters of normal discourse.

The position of the followers of Barth represents in part a theological reaction to the sort of pressure that theism has been put under by the philosophical school associated with Ayer, 'logical positivism'. They have tried to take on board Ayer's claim that theological language is meaningless, but have made of this meaninglessness a kind of superior divine logic. Indeed, they have found that such an approach protects the believer from criticism. They admit that theology is meaningless to those outside the realm of faith ('faith' being interpreted as a direct transmission of knowledge to the individual, who acquires understanding on the basis of a kind of spiritual drip-feed connecting God with the believer). They therefore feel that their 'secular' critics have nothing significant to say to them. In effect, Ayer has put them in a ghetto and they are happy to remain there, content to be making statements of nonsense in the assurance that what to the believer are the words of God must necessarily appear to the unbeliever mere gobbledygook.

On the other hand, there are those on both sides whom I would label 'meaning' theists and 'meaning' atheists, between whom a dialogue about God's existence can take place. 'Meaning' theists do not claim that on the basis of some special gift from God, 'faith' or 'grace' or 'revelation', they are able to be assured that God exists whilst being quite unable to communicate the grounds of their assurance to others who lack this divine gift. 'Meaning' atheists do not make the claim that language about God is incommunicable either — in their case because they do not regard it as emanating from a philosophical No Go area labelled 'metaphysics' that is pronounced to be beyond the bounds of sense. 'Meaning' theists and 'meaning' atheists are able to accept that a common definition of 'God' can be found and the evidence for and against God's existence duly weighed and argued over.

In order to advance the debate about God, we need to presume that this debate is between 'meaning' theists and 'meaning' atheists. But perhaps this is something we presume for our own convenience. What is the evidence that the argument of the 'no meaning' theists and the 'no meaning' atheists is an incorrect one? In the next two sections I shall examine more closely the positions outlined by Ayer and Barth.

'no meaning' atheists

Language, Truth and Logic makes the 'no meaning' atheist position clear in its first chapter, 'The Elimination of Metaphysics':

> Our charge against the metaphysician is not that he attempts to employ the understanding in a field where it cannot possibly venture, but that he produces sentences which fail to conform to the conditions under which alone a sentence can be literally significant.

So the argument against the theist is that he or she does not produce a meaningful sentence when talking about God. The conditions under which sentences can be 'literally significant' are not met. But what are the conditions? And are they the right conditions?

Ayer tells us in the next paragraph:

> The criterion which we use to test the genuineness of apparent statements of fact is the criterion of verifiability. We say that a sentence is factually significant to any given person if, and only if, he knows how to verify the proposition which it purports to express — that is, if he knows what observations would lead him, under certain conditions, to accept the proposition as being true, or reject it as being false.

Ayer gives us an example of what he considers to be a meaningless theological statement: 'The Absolute enters into, but is itself incapable of, evolution and progress'. Because, he claims, 'one cannot conceive of an observation which would enable one to determine whether the Absolute did, or did not, enter into evolution and progress', then whoever makes a theological statement like the one above 'has made an utterance which has no literal significance even for himself'.

In one sense Ayer's claim seems reasonable. If anyone claims to be making a factual statement, then they ought to be able to state what observations would be relevant to determining the truth or falsity of that statement. But then, many theists would claim that theological statements filled this bill perfectly well. Take the statement 'God made the world'. A theist might claim that there were a number of observations that were relevant to determining the truth or falsity of that statement. For instance, he or she might make observations about the beauty of the natural world or the complexity of its design, and claim that these were evidence of the existence of a divine Creator. Such claims might be contentious, but it would be odd to see them as meaningless.

Even the rather unwieldy theological statement quoted by Ayer could be interpreted in this way. A Christian would argue that the life of Christ represents the Absolute 'entering into' human history, whilst denying that this meant God Himself was subject to change. The claim would be that Jesus of Nazareth represented observable evidence of the divine nature.

Ayer's response to this argument would be to agree that natural beauty, the intricacy of the physical universe, or the short life of a Galilean Jew, represented observable evidence. But he would deny that they were evidence of God. In another passage from *Language, Truth and Logic* he writes:

> ...If the sentence 'God exists' entails no more than that certain types of phenomena occur in certain sequences, then to assert the existence of a god will be simply equivalent to asserting that there is the requisite regularity in nature; and no religious man would admit that this was all he intended to assert in asserting the existence of a god.

Ayer begins, then, by arguing that anyone claiming to make a factual statement must be capable of saying what observations would count towards establishing the truth or falsity of that statement. Then the theist offers examples of observations which he or she would claim count for (or conceivably against) the existence of God. But now Ayer claims that these observations have no meaning as evidence for the existence of a god. Thus when the theist says 'regularity in nature is evidence of God's existence', Ayer replies: 'All you are saying is that there's regularity in nature'. But has he any right to tell the theist this? After all, the theist is seeking to conform with the verification principle and is listing observations which count for or against God's existence. If Ayer then tells the theist that he or she is still unable to make meaningful theological statements, then it cannot surely be on the basis of the verification principle, the principle by which he claims to distinguish meaningful from meaningless statements. He is, of course, entitled to deny that regularity in nature establishes or counts for the existence of a god. But is he entitled on the basis of his own principle to continue to say: 'Theological statements are meaningless'?

A general reading of the book encourages the suspicion that the principle of verification is being used, not simply to exclude some clear and obvious errors, but to cut out swathes of philosophical tradition that have never been guilty of the crude misconceptions of which they are accused by Ayer.

Thus, in his chapter 'The Elimination of Metaphysics', Ayer cites a number of philosophical problems which he believes can be rapidly cleared up through a proper understanding of language. He believes that the use of the term 'substance' is a good example:

It happens to be the case that we cannot, in our language, refer to the sensible properties of a thing without introducing a word or phrase which appears to stand for the thing itself as opposed to anything which may be said about it.

The metaphysician, 'misled by a superficial grammatical feature of his language', thereby supposes, Ayer argues, that the thing itself is a simple entity, which can be distinguished from its attributes. The metaphysician uses the word 'substance' of the 'thing itself', and thinks of its various properties as attached to it in much the same way that garments become attached to a clothes horse. The 'thing itself', the 'substance', is thought of as an object that can be separated from its attributes. It somehow 'lies beneath' them as another 'thing', much as the clothes horse lies underneath the clothes.

Ayer identifies here an error made by some philosophers. But his own position, which is that an entity can simply be defined in terms of 'the totality of its appearances', is similarly questionable. Ayer claims that 'logical analysis' (whatever that is) shows that what makes these 'appearances' the 'appearances of' the same thing is not their relationship to an entity other than themselves, but their relationship to one another. In fact only *some* logical analysis shows this. Most philosophers recognise the fallacy of the clothes horse view of the 'thing itself'. But they do not necessarily conclude that a thing is no more than the sum of its attributes. They agree that the clothes horse analogy is too crude a way of conveying the relationship between what a thing is and the fact that it is. But a philosophical tradition stretching back to Aristotle's exploration of the relationship between 'first substance' and 'second substance' in *The Categories* has seen that there are other ways of exploring the issue.

Much the same can be said of Ayer's treatment of existence.

A simpler and clearer instance of the way in which a consideration of grammar leads to metaphysics is the case of the metaphysical concept of Being.

Here again, he concludes that there is a simple misunderstanding of language. The statements 'Martyrs exist' and 'Martyrs suffer' both contain a noun followed by an intransitive verb. We therefore might be misled into thinking that they are of the same logical type. But this would be wrong because, as Kant has demonstrated, 'existence is not an attribute', an additional property which a thing has on top of its other properties like greenness, tallness, or roundness.

Once again, Ayer highlights an error that some philosophers have made, and which Anselm certainly made in his famous argument for the existence of God (which I will examine later). But most of the philosophers who have written about and explored the nature of being have not been so crude. They have seen that, in the words of the philosopher G.E. Moore, there is a difference between the way in which the word 'exist' is used in the sentence 'tame tigers exist', and the way in which the word 'growl' is used in the sentence 'tame tigers growl'. But they have not concluded that it is a useless and mistaken speculative enterprise to consider what it means to say that something 'exists'. To argue that much of the work of philosophers like Aristotle or theologians like Aquinas was based on a simple grammatical error is quite unfair.

What *Language, Truth and Logic* does is to call a particular philosophical position, rather than a particular branch of philosophy, 'metaphysics' and thereby nonsense. Ayer takes a number of issues examined by all philosophers as part of a broad introduction to philosophy: What is the self? What does it mean to say that something exists? What is an object? He then attacks certain answers to these questions as 'metaphysics'. He identifies some real errors based on misunderstanding of language, but then reduces all philosophical positions other than his own to such errors. As a result an enormous amount of philosophy is scorned and rejected. In dismissing metaphysics, Ayer is not dismissing an old-fashioned and unnecessary part of philosophy. He is trying to exclude a particular approach to many central problems of philosophy. The question of God's existence is merely one of these central problems.

It is, then, into a more general reductive process that we would place Ayer's treatment of God. Later in this book, when discussing the divine nature, ideas of existence and of the self that have been part of the debate over theism will be discussed. There is some similarity between these issues, particularly when it is borne in mind that the theist does not regard God as a supra-terrestrial object for whose existence or non-existence no earthly observations could conceivably be of relevance. The theist denies that the boundaries of heaven begin where the boundaries of earth end. Any theist committed to the view that God is omnipresent must by definition believe that there is evidence of God's presence in the reality observed on earth. Ayer can, of course, claim that this reality can be understood without recourse to theism. He can do so in just the way that he believes the totality of appearances can be interpreted without belief in 'substances', or that there is no further significance to existence than that it is not a predicate. But can the verification principle give him the right to do this, when those who take a different view from him feel entitled to claim that they are abiding by that principle? Cannot they too be committed to the view that philosophy must deal with matters of fact, and that to claim something as a matter of fact one must be able to state what observations would in principle establish its truth or falsity? Certainly Ayer has a different view of what facts can be construed from those observations than they do. But can he use that difference to call his opponents' view 'metaphysics' and therefore nonsense? Is he sweeping the pieces off the chess-board rather than engaging in the game?

As a 'no meaning' atheist, Ayer attempts to find a principle in terms of which to reject the whole business of theology as meaningless. I have tried to argue that the principle does not succeed in this task, and moreover that a great deal of philosophy would also be rejected by Ayer's approach. If Ayer's position were correct, then the argument between theists and atheists could proceed no further. But what I have tried to show is that a theist could actually claim to be abiding by the Verification Principle when making statements about God. Those statements may be true or false, but there is nothing in their form to exclude them at the outset from consideration.

'no meaning' theists

'No meaning' theists make particular use of theological terms that point to a special kind of knowledge delivered to the believer by God. Words such as 'revelation', 'grace', and in particular 'faith' are enlisted in order to justify the idea of an exclusive channel of communication between the Deity and His followers. In reality these terms have been interpreted in a number of different ways.

I have already mentioned the influence of Barth in the modern day. This section looks back further into Christian tradition and examines the concept of faith, particularly in relation to the word which it is so often contrasted to, 'reason', in order to identify more clearly the stance adopted by the 'no meaning' theist.

Before beginning to look in detail at an aspect of a particular religious tradition, the Christian tradition, one further point must be made clear. When considering the nature of God in later chapters, I set out to include consideration of a range of world religions. In this first chapter, however, the illustrations are limited to the Judaeo-Christian tradition. Since the purpose of this chapter is, as I have said, a preamble to the discussion of God's nature, the limitation of scope is not perhaps too serious. When it comes to asking who or what theists consider God to be, on the other hand, any answer must embrace as far as it can the full spectrum of religious opinion. In later chapters, then, I hope that I will display a more ecumenical perspective than I manage in this one!

To a Christian, the word 'faith' will probably recall the arguments of the Protestant Reformation and the debate about the idea of 'justification by faith' which has dominated much of Christian history since that time. The Protestant Reformers argued that salvation was earned by faith and not by 'works' — good deeds. But they then had to contend with the response that faith itself might be interpreted as an 'inner work', a good deed of the mind. They therefore adopted the view that faith was not a work because it was an act of God rather than of the human person. Whereas works were human actions, faith was a gift of grace, a divine action, something implanted in the believer by God — the sort of imagery that Barth refined in his work on Anselm.

Naturally enough, this view of faith as a divine gift rather than the product of a human effort was used to mark off the believers from the unbelievers. Some people were given faith; some people were not. It was a fact of life. To John Calvin, among others, it simply proved that God had pre-destined some to eternal salvation and some to eternal damnation before they were born.

Ask a Christian why he or she believes that God exists, and they might reply: 'It is a matter of faith.' Otherwise the questioner wouldn't need to ask the question. If the questioner persists by saying: 'At least explain to me what it's like to believe in God', they will refuse the offer once again. Faith only speaks to faith. To those outside, it is all nonsense — an observation that Ayer would be the first to corroborate.

John Wesley discussed faith in these terms when he compared it to a 'spiritual sense' in his *Earnest Appeal to Men of Reason and Religion:*

> .....as you cannot reason concerning colours if you have no natural sight — because all the ideas received by your senses are of a different kind...so you cannot reason concerning spiritual things if you have no spiritual sight, because all your ideas received by your outward senses are of a different kind....

Wesley has an explanation of why the believer cannot explain to the unbeliever what he or she has learned by faith. It would be like explaining to someone blind what colour is like. Once again, Ayer's position proves convenient to this sort of theist. He is the blind man who cannot see, like many others described in the Christian gospels. Of course colour-talk (metaphysical language) appears nonsense to him. It is outside the range of his sense-experience.

When Christians in this tradition talk of reason, on the other hand, they dismiss it as a human work, tainted therefore by sin and liable to mislead. They see the 'cunning' of the serpent in the Garden of Eden as the wiles of the first intellectual (probably a theologian). The Christian who puts his or her trust in reason commits the folly of hubris, putting faith in something that is human. Reason has a role, but only when doing the work of faith. It articulates what is revealed by the sixth sense. Even in this limited role, however, reason is liable to cause trouble to the faithful, because such articulation requires that the lines of communication between believer and unbeliever are re-opened. So long as it maintains the idea that believers talking to unbelievers are like people explaining to the blind what it is like to see, reason may be tolerated. But even the blind can make certain demands for consistency upon those with sight.

I cannot examine here the way in which this view of religious knowledge can be paralleled within other traditions (in the eighth century A.D., for instance, there was a debate within Islam along lines similar to the sixteenth-century Christian debate over faith and works). Nor can I look at the way in which this view of faith and reason has influenced contemporary Christian thinking, both mainstream and among the evangelical or fundamentalist groups where it is most in evidence. What I want to concentrate upon are the different models used in order to explain basic theological terms. Wesley's model for explaining the nature of faith is the model of perception. Those with faith are those who can 'see', and who may therefore only engage in a limited dialogue with the 'blind'. There are limits to what they can say in explaining their beliefs, the sort of limits which we tend to accept when imagining the constraints upon giving a blind person some understanding of what the world looks like (although, as said, it would be wrong to suppose that we could communicate nothing in such circumstances). Such a model attempts to encourage the unbeliever to excuse the believer from the task of justifying theism. It seeks to make clear that the task is bound to be an impossibility, because the unbeliever lacks the God-given capacity to understand.

This model of faith is clearly very comfortable for the believer. As a 'no meaning' theist, he or she is protected from the sort of self-criticism that must come when believer and unbeliever are challenging one another on common ground. But many believers will say that such comfort is precisely what faith is meant to give them. They might accept that they *are* a privileged group, receiving an assurance that frees them to act in the world without fear and uncertainty. In the context of a thorough-going twentieth-century challenge to religious belief, it is easy to see how this kind of retreat to a self-contained theism becomes attractive.

Yet this position cannot be sustained. Any claim to 'special knowledge' through faith or revelation or grace cannot avoid the task of explaining just what this knowledge is knowledge of. Any claim to direct acquaintance with God through immediate religious experience has to explain what the experience is experience of. Ayer makes this point in discussing what he calls 'mysticism'. I cannot be refuted if I claim that my visual sense-field contains a yellow sense-content, but I can be refuted if I go on to claim that there exists a yellow object that is responsible for my sense-content. Similarly, I cannot be refuted if I claim to experience a religious emotion. But if I claim that my religious experience is experience of God, then I am not simply talking about my own feelings but about a transcendent being that I am claiming my feelings to be feelings of. Therefore, I can no longer be allowed to escape criticism and analysis of my theistic views on the grounds that they are simply a matter of personal experience. It does not matter whether I claim that God has granted me special revelation, a unique experience, or an unshakeable conviction which I choose to call 'faith'. In each case, if I am to claim that this revelation or experience is of 'God', and is not simply an expression of some form of mental delusion which should be referred to a psychoanalyst, then I am forced to debate the interpretation that I am giving. This is the key point. 'No meaning' theists talk of 'self-authenticating experiences'. That is fine. But to say that my experience is 'experience of God' is to move beyond the experience to give a particular interpretation of it. What is self-authenticating is the fact that I have had an experience. But to say that I have had an experience of God, whom I claim to be a transcendent being outside myself, cannot be self-authenticating. For this is to understand my experience in a certain way, a way that others can challenge and ask me to explain.

The 'no meaning' atheist denies that the theist can state what observations would lead him or her to accept as true, or deny as false, the proposition that 'God exists'. The 'no meaning' theist denies that the theist needs to say anything about the existence of God that is intelligible to those who don't already accept the existence of God as true. I have found neither position acceptable. But there is the other form both of theism and of atheism — the 'meaning' form. In the next section we shall look at the position of theists and of atheists when they do not rule out the possibility of dialogue with one another on grounds of unintelligibility, whether the unintelligibility be God-given or humanly made.

the dilemma of 'meaning theism'

If we accept the position either of the 'no meaning' theist or the 'no meaning' atheist, then the debate cannot proceed any further. But in the case of 'meaning theism' and 'meaning atheism' it can do. Since the presumption of both 'meaning' theist and 'meaning' atheist is that each can understand and criticise what the other is saying, the main arguments for and against theism can be brought out by following through the position of either. My own inquiry into God will try to make sense of the 'meaning' theist position, but in doing so I shall also be making clear — since they encounter one another on common ground — what the view of the 'meaning' atheist might be.

In the last section we found the 'no meaning' theist employing terms like 'faith' to suggest an exclusive mode of communication between God and the believer. A very different view of faith is the one explored by John Locke in *The Reasonableness of Christianity*. Locke's late seventeenth-century confidence in reason represented precisely the sort of view that Wesley's eighteenth-century religious revival was designed to subvert. Where Wesley stressed faith as a gift of God, Locke stressed reason as a gift of God. It is reason, he argued, that is the distinguishing feature of human beings as against other examples of creation. It should therefore be particularly revered. And Locke warned against 'giving up reason for revelation', which he associated with 'enthusiasm' (a word that around 1700 meant 'fanaticism').

It is clear that for Locke the perception model of faith created an unsatisfactory barrier between those with faith and those without. He recognised that some understanding is given directly by God, but also that it has to be appropriated by human beings using their reason. To give up reason for revelation, he argued, is 'like putting out one's eyes in order to look through a telescope'. In another passage he argued that 'God when he makes the prophet does not unmake the man' — in other words God leaves the prophet with his faculties intact in order to judge the prophecy.

For Locke the separate compartments for faith and reason, or reason and revelation, did not exist. Reason he defined as 'natural revelation'. Revelation he defined as 'natural reason enlarged'. Faith is 'a firm assent of the mind', for which there should be good reason. As the title of his book indicated, the Christian faith should be a 'reasonable' faith.

However, many Christians nowadays, even though they might admire and approve of Locke's preparedness to make faith reasonable, would not be happy with the particular arguments he used to establish that reasonableness. He has a confidence, typical of his time, that the works of nature provide sufficient evidence of a Deity. He believed that the teachings of Christ gather together the wisdom of the ages into one source, and present it for the 'uneducated' along with a few miracles in order to win their attention and support (much as the outlaw in the Western uses his gun in order to win an audience in a crowded saloon bar). For Locke, it was possible from reason alone to know that there is a God, and the role of revelation tended to be seen as a way to produce belief among those whose reason was undeveloped. The Incarnation became a way of instructing the poor and ignorant in truths long since grasped by the wise and philosophically educated! Such snobbery perhaps helps to explain some of the support which the Wesleyan tradition must have engendered, among people who found the 'spiritual sense' of faith a way of rebutting the patronising condescension of the 'men of reason'.

Wesley and Locke represent the dilemma perceived in religion by many during the modern period of the Enlightenment. On the one hand there is the position of the 'no meaning' theist, occupied by those who talk of faith in the way that Wesley talked of it. They are certainly comfortable and assured, but at the same time they have no real chance of converting others to their views, at least if conversion means more than expressing the hope that God will send faith to others too. So far as talking is concerned, they can only do it to each other.

On the other hand, there are those like Locke who belong to the best traditions of the Age of Reason and represent the 'meaning' theist position. They are convinced that religion must make sense to believer and unbeliever alike. They admit that the truths of revelation or of faith must be accessible to reason. As Locke said, 'Tis no diminishing to revelation, that reason gives its suffrage too, to the truths revelation has discovered.' But those in this tradition wildly overestimated the friendliness towards revelation that human reason would feel, once freed from the shackles of a state compulsion to believe. They had a cosy assurance in the obvious existence of a divine architect for what they took to be an elegant and attractive world, neatly designed like one of their drawing-rooms. They understood faith to be an assent of the mind as agreeable to reason as assenting to the existence of objects on a table. And they still relied on traditional arguments about the authority of Scripture in order to establish certain beliefs that were 'above' although not 'contrary to' reason, for instance resurrection of the dead. Once the nineteenth century had begun to let Darwin and Biblical Criticism loose on these twin pillars of their 'reasonable faith', it proved eminently easy to dislodge. From the point of view of many who have traced the development of religious thought over the last two hundred years, theism ceased to be unshakeable long before, in the twentieth century, Ayer and others from the school of 'logical positivism' sought to make it impossible.

There has, however, been another tradition of thought associated neither with the 'rationalism' of Locke nor the 'fideism' of Wesley. This tradition belongs neither to the Age of Reason nor (in Wesley's sense) to the age of faith. It is a tradition that has refused to claim the certainty claimed by both these camps. It has neither Locke's confidence in reason nor Wesley's confidence in his spiritual sense. Unlike Wesley, it engages with the unbeliever on common ground. Unlike Locke, it does not possess the assurance of having won the argument on that ground. Its position is that of the 'meaning' theist, but it does not claim the certainty of God's existence with which that position is often associated.

'meaning theism' and the uncertainty principle

The idea that the theist must be certain of God's existence deserves careful consideration. This matter is important partly because of the particular status in religious thought of ideas that God's existence can be 'proved'. It is also significant because critics of theism have sometimes claimed that theists wish their statements about God to be 'necessary' propositions — propositions whose denial involves a contradiction. It has been pointed out that the only propositions of which this is true are 'analytic' propositions — those that contain not statements of fact but rules about language. It is, therefore, claimed that the desire of the theist to make a necessarily true statement of fact is impossible. The presumption behind such arguments is that theists wish their statements about God to be propositions that it would be impossible to deny. Yet if the theist is prepared to admit that he or she does not have to be certain of the truths that they are affirming, this particular criticism of theism fails.

One of the most common complaints against theists by philosophers is that they will not say what would count against their belief in God. In a well-known collection of essays, *New Essays in Philosophical Theology*, Antony Flew argues that believers will never answer the question: What event or series of events would provide sufficient evidence against the existence of God to stop you believing? Flew thinks that nothing would. Believers will believe in God whatever happens on earth. Even a father who watches his son dying of cancer will go on believing that God is a loving father. For Flew, and for Ayer in *Language, Truth and Logic*, you realise the vacuousness of religious belief when you realise that it is compatible with any earthly state of affairs whatsoever.

In that same collection of essays, however, an interesting parable is advanced in response to Flew by the philosopher of religion Basil Mitchell. The parable is as follows: In an occupied country during wartime, a member of the resistance meets a stranger who deeply impresses him, and who assures him that he is on the side of the resistance. The partisan feels that he can trust the stranger, although that trust is tested in future weeks. Sometimes the stranger appears in the uniform of the police handing over other partisans to the forces of occupation. At other times he engages in activities that help the resistance. The evidence for the stranger's allegiance is therefore ambiguous, and Mitchell makes clear that the partisan's trust in him is not unconditional. Nevertheless, Mitchell points out that it is of the nature of commitment to come to terms with what may count against one's own beliefs as well as what may count for them.

Mitchell's parable is specifically designed to reflect upon the problem of God's love in the face of evil, rather than of God's existence. Nevertheless, its point about the evidence for God's goodness — that it is not compelling and that, indeed, there may be moments when it appears that the facts of life may not be reconciled with a good Creator at all — might also be applied to the evidence for God's existence. In both cases, one could make the point against Flew that the believer does not accept that nothing would count against his or her belief in God. Of course, certain things do. Many people indeed have decided not to believe because of experiencing the sort of suffering that Flew identifies with the frantic father whose son is dying. Believers very often cease to believe because such suffering makes them no longer able to accept the goodness of God. There is no reason to suppose that they might not also be swayed to reject the existence of God because of particular events or even of particular arguments.

The position we might adopt against Flew is this. You are too used to dealing with theists who adopt a position of unassailable certainty in their beliefs. For them it may be right to say that no conceivable circumstance in their lives would change the nature of their convictions. But is that necessarily the only theistic position? Could not the theist argue that faith in God is a form of trust like that which, in Mitchell's parable, is placed in the stranger by the partisan? If it is of this form, then by definition there will be facts and events that will count against it. Indeed it could be argued that if there were nothing to count against it then it would no longer be faith!

Flew might say: But would anything count finally against it? Would anything actually convert belief in God into disbelief? Again, I see no reason why the theist should not reply that in principle, yes, there might be events that would 'de-convert' the believer. There is, after all, such a thing in religious tradition as loss of faith, which may be prompted by experience of personal tragedy or by reading a particularly convincing argument against theism. Just as the partisan might eventually lose his faith in the stranger, so the theist might lose his or her faith in God.

The sense in which I use the word 'faith' here is different from both Wesley and Locke. For Wesley faith is a spiritual sense somehow implanted in the self by God that is ineradicable once received. It provides a certainty that God exists which is on a par with the sort of certainty we claim from our sense-experience. It is a direct intuition of God, in effect a hotline that bypasses the ambiguous world of the senses that might indeed provide only partial or uncertain evidence of the Deity. For Locke, faith is a form of intellectual assent to propositions, some of which are the conclusion of reasoned argument and some of which are the product of acceptance of revelation (as assessed by reason). Once again, faith is understood as offering certainty, in this case what might be called 'intellectual certainty', the consequence of accepting that a particular line of argument is overwhelmingly convincing.

Locke's enthusiasm is alive and well in the modern day too, despite the buffeting religious belief has had in the West over the last two hundred years. Take, for instance, the following discussion, first broadcast in 1948 by BBC radio, between the atheist Bertrand Russell and the Jesuit theologian F.C. Copleston. Their debate on the existence of God opened as follows:

> COPLESTON: As we are going to discuss the existence of God, it might perhaps be as well to come to some provisional agreement as to what we understand by the term 'God'. I presume that we mean a supreme personal being — distinct from the world and creator of the world. Would you agree — provisionally at least — to accept this statement as the meaning of the term 'God'?
> RUSSELL: Yes, I accept this definition.
> COPLESTON: Well, my position is the affirmative position that such a being actually exists, and that His existence can be proved philosophically. Perhaps you would tell me if your position is that of agnosticism or of atheism. I mean, would you say that the non-existence of God can be proved?
> RUSSELL: No, I should not say that. My position is agnostic.

Copleston believed that the theist must be able to prove the existence of God. Russell rejected theism on the grounds that the existence of God can neither be proven nor disproven. But was Russell's position any less compatible with faith in God than Copleston's?

Let us concede (what in fact should not be conceded) that a proof that God existed would make the theist certain of God's existence. Is it not possible to find an understanding of faith that is compatible with uncertainty rather than certainty of the existence of a Deity? In ordinary language, the word 'faith' is used in a quite different sense from that used by either Wesley or Locke and Copleston. If I say: 'I have faith in you to post this letter', such a statement is compatible only with an intellectual uncertainty that you will do so. If I actually follow you down the street in order to be sure that you don't throw it away or forget to post it, for instance, then I at one and the same time become certain that you've posted it and display a *lack* of faith that you will do so. Faith here means a commitment to believe in the face of evidence that is accepted as ambiguous, like the commitment of the partisan in the face of the ambiguous behaviour of the stranger in Mitchell's parable.

It is noticeable that the Russell-Copleston debate became embroiled in a discussion of necessary propositions, a discussion made necessary by Copleston's desire to show Russell that the world is such that it *must* be the case that it has a Creator. But does theism have to make such a case? Isn't it making the mistake of claiming too much? Isn't it unnecessarily raising the stakes here? Do we really have to be sure that God exists in order to believe in God? Cannot we argue, indeed, on the basis of the usual meaning of 'faith' that involves trust in the face of intellectual *un*certainty, that Russell's uncertainty as to whether or not God exists, the agnostic position, is the one the theist in fact should hold?

Suppose there existed a God who wished us to be unsure whether or not He existed. Could we not, for instance, suggest that this God felt human beings would only be able to show the sort of moral commitment that He considered desirable if they were uncertain that He existed? He would prefer us to be in the position of the person who learns to trust that a friend has posted a letter, and who does not go out to be certain that the letter has found its destination, a search that in fact would portray not faith, but a lack of faith. God might, in creating the world, have put the sort of distance between Himself and ourselves that involves our having to live in an environment within which, until the day that we die, there is evidence both for and against His existence. If we nevertheless believe that He exists, we are only showing the sort of commitment that the partisan shows. We are not claiming to be able to prove His existence. We are not claiming either that He has somehow implanted in us a sixth sense that gives us certainty He exists whilst our other five senses provide no such assurance.

The position I have attempted to outline in this first chapter is that of the 'meaning' theist, but it is also that of the 'meaning' atheist. I am arguing that a common ground exists between theists and atheists, where each exchanges different interpretations of reality and understands each other's views. They may reach different conclusions, but they do not pre-empt the discussion by claiming either that one side is talking nonsense or that the other side is talking from a position of impossible disadvantage through lack of faith. Of course this common ground automatically implies a battle. It means that there will be a lack of certainty on both sides. The theist will encounter doubts about the correctness of his or her belief, while the atheist will encounter similar doubts about disbelief. Both theists and atheists have often seen a position such as this as too volatile to be credible. Neither side feels that its principles may be maintained if it is tempted by the other. But need this be so?

In the next chapter I examine further the idea that believers in God may be less than certain of God's existence. A number of important examples from the history of religious thought help us to probe further the nature of religious belief. Can it bear the interpretation which I have tried to place upon it?

notes

Ayer, Alfred Born in 1910, he did more than anyone else to familiarise the Anglo-Saxon world with the twentieth-century school of thought known as 'logical positivism', particularly through the best-seller, *Language, Truth and Logic*. Most of Ayer's life has been spent teaching philosophy at London and Oxford. Few philosophers have been able to match his clarity and lucidity (although Antony Flew, an equally committed atheist and twentieth-century philosopher, must come close).

Barth, Karl (1886-1968) A Swiss theologian of immense reputation (known in some circles as a Protestant Aquinas!), Karl Barth was fundamentally a traditionalist thinker. The school of thought associated with him — 'neo-orthodoxy' — is essentially an attempt to re-present the 'orthodoxy' of the Protestant Reformation in twentieth-century terms.

Locke, John (1632-1704) An English philosopher who in the context of his time (and of his own life which involved a period of exile) was a clear defender of toleration and free enquiry. His work, *The Reasonableness of Christianity,* is still a classic in the philosophy of religion.

Russell, Bertrand (1872-1970) One of the most famous modern philosophers, Bertrand Russell was also an active peace campaigner as a deeply committed supporter of CND. His work, *Principia Mathematica*, jointly written with Alfred North Whitehead, is one of the most influential philosophical writings of the twentieth century, but he also wrote clear and accessible introductory works. His short book, *The Problems of Philosophy*, is still an excellent introduction to the subject.

Wesley, John (1703-1791) Regarded (despite his own desire to remain within the Anglican Church) as the founder of Methodism. A man of both charisma and personal piety, John Wesley is a legendary figure for his tireless travels around the country on horseback, preaching at every opportunity (often in the open air, largely because he was banned from using pulpits). More religious thinker than systematic theologian (more a Luther than a Calvin), Wesley's ideas cannot easily be defined, although his faith was clearly based upon personal experience rather than intellectual conviction.

further reading

A useful collection of extracts and texts, including a helpful introduction, is provided by John Hick in *The Existence of God*, published by the Macmillan Company in 1964 as part of their *Problems of Philosophy* Series. The fascinating debate between Copleston and Russell can be found in this reader, together with short extracts from the history of philosophy concerning the traditional arguments for God's existence. In 1971 Hick published a longer account of his own ideas in *Arguments for the Existence of God.*

The collection of essays entitled *New Essays in Philosophical Theology,* edited by Antony Flew and Alasdair McIntyre, is unmissable and full of ideas. The section on 'Theology and Falsification' has been particularly influential. Antony Flew's atheist position is clearly and pungently stated in his *God and Philosophy.*

2: belief in God

In the last chapter I introduced the 'uncertainty principle', the idea that belief in God was more compatible with a degree of uncertainty that God existed than with certainty of His existence. In this chapter we examine this idea more closely. How uncertain, for instance, can the believer be? Must the existence of God be probable, or can theism seek to defend its position against the improbability of God's existence?

I set out a position which argues that there may be too much and also too little evidence for the existence of God to make religious belief a tenable option. We begin with the argument that the evidence for a Deity might be so strong as to undermine faith. I argue that implicit in the whole religious vocabulary of faith and belief is a condition of trust that is only compatible with intellectual uncertainty. In the following section, on the other hand, I argue that this vocabulary can equally be undermined if the evidence for God's existence is too weak. In such a situation, I suggest, faith becomes blind, belief becomes credulous and trust becomes misplaced. Belief in God can be eroded from two opposite directions — from the effort to prove God's existence on the one hand, and from the denial of any evidence for God's existence on the other. Let us examine each of these in turn.

wagers, ventures and chessboards

We start with a famous passage of the French religious thinker Blaise Pascal's *Thoughts*, in which the seventeenth-century writer compared belief in a God to a bet or wager. 'According to reason', Pascal suggested, 'you cannot bet either way.' But the choice of whether to believe in God is determined by at least one rational consideration. Even if the chance of success in a wager is very slight, the bet should be accepted if the reward of the wager is disproportionately high in relation to the amount staked.

In Pascal's argument, the possibility of God's existence may actually be very slight. However, since the rewards of believing are so high (in fact infinite) in proportion to the amount staked (a finite life), the bet is worth having even when, in all likelihood, it will be lost.

> But here there is an infinity of infinitely happy life to win, one chance of winning against a finite number of chances of losing, and what you stake is finite. That removes all doubt as to choice: wherever the infinite is, and there is not an infinity of chances of loss against the chance of winning, there are no two ways about it, all must be given.

Whatever the level of probability that God exists, in Pascal's view, one should believe in God, one should wager. One should always risk a finite certainty for an infinite uncertainty. A bird in the hand is never worth an infinite number of birds in the bush.

There may be considerable scepticism about Pascal's case for always wagering on the outsider if the odds are high enough. What is interesting, however, is the comparison between belief in God and the kind of risk venture undertaken when making a bet. To Pascal religious belief was a commitment made in a context of obvious intellectual uncertainty. If God's existence is 'wagered upon' in the way that the outcome of a race is wagered upon, then by definition that existence cannot be certainly known until after the race is run (presumably after death). Indeed Pascal's commitment to the outsider would seem to entail that even if the possibility of God's existence were extremely small, the choice of belief should be made. His position could be summed up as saying that so long as it has not been established beyond doubt that God does *not* exist, we should believe in God.

Another writer with a similar argument is the eighteenth-century cleric Bishop Butler. In his *Analogy*, Butler concerned himself with the question of what sort of evidence one must possess in order to believe in God. His central principle was that 'probability is the guide to life', and he applied this principle to those who find it difficult to accept Christianity. His argument was that they expect to be certain, and therefore interpret any doubt as evidence of unbelief:

> They take for granted, that if Christianity were true, the light of it must have been more general, and the evidence of it more satisfactory...if any of these persons are, upon the whole, in doubt concerning the truth of Christianity; their behaviour seems owing to their taking for granted, through strange inattention, that such doubting is, in a manner, the same thing as being certain against it.

It is an old but still neglected adage that doubt is not the opposite of faith but of certainty. Despite the familiar language from the confessional about 'having doubts', there is a tradition within Christianity that refuses to accept that there is any conflict between intellectual doubts (including doubts about the existence of God), and religious belief. Furthermore, that tradition would claim that intellectual doubt was a necessary ingredient of faith, and not simply something faith could 'learn to live with'. Certainty that God existed, or the existence of a convincing 'proof' of the existence of God such as Anselm attempts in the *Proslogion*, would be incompatible with faith in God. The only God that one can have faith in is a God whose existence cannot be demonstrated in the way that a mathematical equation can be demonstrated.

Precisely this point is made by one of the most subtle and underrated religious writers on the philosophy of religion in the nineteenth century, John Henry Newman. Newman argued that as a commitment in the light of evidence that cannot be treated as proof, religious belief is like rather than unlike other forms of belief. There is, however, something of a quantitative scale whereby the more important to us a particular belief may be, the more subtle and even ambiguous will be the evidence for it. He made this clear in his *University Sermons:*

> Next let it be considered, that the following law seems to hold in our attainment of knowledge, that according to its desirableness, whether in point of excellence, or range, or intricacy, so is the subtlety of the evidence on which it is received.

It is the beliefs of which we can be most certain, Newman argues, that play the least significant part in our lives. We can possess a mathematical certainty that two and two make four, but this rarely matters to us. On the other hand, we can never possess such a certainty that someone loves us. There is always a possibility of deceit or self-deception. But it is precisely the possibility of being wrong in believing that someone loves us that makes it appropriate to talk in this context of trust. Where belief in God is concerned, Newman accepted that God's existence can be doubted, and that there is no possibility of the mathematical certainty which can be achieved in the case of equations. But this he regarded as appropriate. The risk of faith is a willingness to venture into what Newman elsewhere called a 'certainty of commitment' without a 'certainty of understanding':

> We are so constituted, that if we insist on being as sure as is conceivable, in every step of our course, we must be content to creep along the ground, and can never soar. If we are intended for great ends, we are called to great hazards; and, whereas we are given absolute certainty in nothing, we must in all things choose between doubt and inactivity, and the conviction that we are under the eye of One who, for whatever reason, exercises us with the less evidence when He might give us the greater.

If we seek to protect ourselves from doubt in matters of belief, the result will be 'inactivity'. The person who seeks to protect himself or herself from doubt in their beliefs, Newman argued, is like the person who, in order to be protected from the risk of illness, never ventures outside the home. Faith is 'a state in which we must assume something to prove anything, and we can gain nothing without venture'. Newman's 'venture', like Pascal's wager, identified belief as a commitment undergone without the certainty of God's existence — indeed a commitment that makes sense only without that certainty.

Pascal, Butler and Newman pointed out in their different ways that religious belief can be endangered by too much evidence for the existence of God — evidence that amounts to proof. But belief may also be threatened from the opposite direction — by too little evidence that there is a God. It is this that we examine in the next section.

ventures are not leaps

There is a school of thought that claims that faith is an act of will made in defiance of the irrationality of believing that God exists.

It recalls a famous saying of the third-century Christian Tertullian: *Credo quia absurdum est* (I believe because it is absurd). It is a position often linked to existentialist religious writers, and particularly to the Danish thinker of the early nineteenth century, often regarded as the founding father of existentialism, Søren Kierkegaard.

This position claims that the existence of God not only cannot be proved but cannot make sense. It would agree with Ayer that so far as reason is concerned, theism is nonsense. But faith, it would say, is a deliberate defiance of what reason says, a leap into the dark that accepts that which it claims is 'absurd' or 'paradoxical'.

The argument we have advanced, however, is different from this. Whether we are talking about Pascal's wager or Newman's venture, we are always talking about a commitment made after weighing evidence. Even the betting person makes a carefully calculated and rational decision about where to put his or her money. The fact that we don't require the evidence of God's existence to be overwhelming does *not* mean that we require no evidence of God's existence at all. The leap of faith may be blind, but the venture of faith is not.

In much existentialist writing the impression is given that, in order to test the believer and evoke real trust, God makes a world in which all the evidence points against Him. An argument of Søren Kierkegaard's expressed this idea in the context of God's goodness, but the idea could equally well be applied to His existence. Kierkegaard highlighted the part of the Old Testament where Abraham is told by God to kill his son Isaac. He prepares to do so, and only when it is clear that he will obey the divine command does God at the last moment spare his son and tell him to kill a sheep instead. Kierkegaard interpreted the parable to mean that we should trust God unconditionally. Even when He appears evil, commanding actions universally regarded as bad such as killing a son, we should nevertheless call Him good. In the same way, we should declare that we believe in the existence of God even when all the evidence is that such belief is absurd. Such absurdity is there only to test our faith in the way that Abraham was tested with an 'absurd' moral demand.

It is doubtful whether Kierkegaard himself held this view, certainly by the time of his last and great work *Concluding Unscientific Postscript,* where he insisted that 'faith must not rest content with unintelligibility'. But some writers have held it, and have welcomed, in a way comparable to the spiritual élitism of the Wesleyan position, the claims that theism is absurd. They see it as a further confirmation of their own moral righteousness in remaining committed to believing in a God who their reason tells them cannot exist.

This position I would resist. I have certainly tried to argue that it makes sense to talk of God inviting trust by withholding the sort of evidence which might admit of certainty that He exists. I am employing the kind of argument that has been used to resist demands that God prove Himself by miraculous interventions of some form — demands that in Christian tradition Christ himself refused to satisfy when he turned down the Pharisees' request for a 'sign' and asked that they have faith instead. But at the same time, to argue that the trust becomes greater, and the faith more admirable, in proportion as the evidence for God becomes slighter, is not our position.

All our discussions of faith as trust, venture or wager have accepted that to subscribe to theism must represent a reasonable commitment on the part of the believer. To revert to the trivial example of the letter posting: one would be willing to applaud the lack of certainty accepted by the person who resists the temptation to follow someone down the street and check whether a letter has been posted. On the other hand, were every indication to be that there was no chance of the letter ever being posted — for example if the person was a known thief and there was no post-box within a hundred miles — then in this case giving him or her the letter would be regarded as stupid. The point is this: trust is only applauded when it is not seen to be misplaced. The fact that believing in God involves an acceptance of uncertainty does not allow us to accept *any* degree of uncertainty, or that trust will also be misplaced.

I am not, then, when I claim that the existence of God does not need to be proved, denying that we must show it to be reasonable to believe in God. The 'leap of faith' argument will not do. Faith ceases to be laudable when it is blind faith. What I try to do in this book is to show that faith is reasonable. I want to argue that it is reasonable to believe in God. In order to do so I do not feel that it is necessary to 'prove' the existence of God in the sense of demonstrating with mathematical certainty that He exists. On the other hand, unless there is some evidence of the existence of God then positive arguments about the need to trust a Deity become negative arguments about credulous and uncritical behaviour.

'meaning theism', 'no meaning theism' and the pursuit of certainty

In the previous two sections I have attempted to outline ways in which the evidence for God's existence may either be too strong or too weak to make sense of religious belief. My conclusions, however, connect up with the discussion of 'meaning' and 'no meaning' forms of theism and atheism in the first chapter. In the approach of the 'no meaning' theist, as I have outlined it above, we can now observe a pursuit of religious certainty that undermines faith. The 'no meaning' theist, always seeks too much evidence of God's existence. The 'meaning' theist, on the other hand, may sometimes claim to need too little — as in the case of the existentialist approach outlined in the last section. But in the case of 'meaning theism' there is the possibility of recognising that the evidence of God's existence may be less than overwhelming without being negligible. The 'meaning' theist is capable of recognising that he or she considers the problem in a mutual dialogue with the 'meaning' atheist, that each is out to convince the other and that each may convert the other to his or her views. That is precisely the sort of vulnerable intellectual position which the 'meaning' theist defends. From his or her point of view this is part of a divinely willed vulnerability through which God elicits a response of commitment from the believer that intellectual uncertainty alone can give.

When the 'meaning' theist believes, he or she lives within and reacts to the same world as the unbeliever. His or her belief, as we have defined it, does not rest upon privileged insight into a supernatural reality hidden from the unbeliever. The 'spiritual sense' view of faith has given rise to a form of spiritual élitism in which the believer welcomes a position in which he or she has no common ground with the unbeliever, and thereby turns the sort of dismissive 'religious language is nonsense' approach of Ayer into a welcome acceptance of the divide between men and women of reason on the one hand, and those with faith on the other. Belief in God, as I have tried to outline it, is a venture, a practical commitment, undergone in acceptance of the fact that the evidence for God's existence is never going to produce certainty. It cannot yield what Newman calls 'proofs such as absolutely to make doubt impossible'.

There is, where the question of God's existence is concerned, an unwillingness on the part of some unbelievers to concede the evidence for theism, and an unwillingness on the part of some believers to concede the limitations of that evidence. Both positions feed off each other. The believer wants to see too much evidence for God — like Copleston, he or she wants proof — and hence the unbeliever sees no evidence. The unbeliever supposes that the believer must have proofs of the existence of God (as we point out below, there is some disagreement over whether some of the traditional 'proofs' of God's existence were intended as proofs at all). And the believer agrees all too easily that he or she must indeed have this sort of proof if belief is to be possible. The believer then claims *either* the sort of reasoned proof in which Locke had confidence, *or* some sort of self-authenticating 'proof from experience' such as Wesley argued for. Neither side will concede the real ambiguity in the evidence, ambiguity which would make the believer uncomfortable in his or her faith, and the unbeliever open to doubt in his or her unwillingness to believe.

In contrast to these ideas about belief and unbelief, the position that I am advocating has few more eloquent supporters than Bishop Blougram in the poet Robert Browning's 'Bishop Blougram's Apology':

Now wait, my friend: well, I do not believe —
If you'll accept no faith that is not fixed,
Absolute and exclusive, as you say.

And now what are we? Unbelievers both,
Calm and complete, determinately fixed
Today, tomorrow and for ever, pray?
You'll guarantee me that? Not so, I think!
In no wise! all we've gained is, that belief,

> As unbelief before, shakes us by fits,
> Confounds us like its predecessor...
>
> All we have gained then by our unbelief
> Is a life of doubt diversified by faith,
> For one of faith diversified by doubt:
> We called the chess-board white, — we call it black.

Blougram does not suggest that there is no difference between belief and unbelief. He suggests that each is more tempted by the other, and more alive to the nature of the other, than either likes to admit. Both have some idea of how reality might come to be perceived as the other perceives it, and both perhaps at times experience in themselves, as an exception what the other experiences as a rule — a life of faith diversified by doubt, or one of doubt diversified by faith. This seems to me to be a more accurate picture of the nature of religious belief than one which suggests that those who *really* believe, must confess to an unbridgeable gulf between themselves and 'unbelief'. There can be no exclusion zone around belief, whether it is put there by believers claiming special enlightenment or philosophers drawing the bounds to sense.

I would not, therefore, expect theism to have to rest its case on the sort of argument for God's existence that Anselm advanced in the eleventh century and which has come to be known as the 'Ontological Argument'. Anselm defined God as 'that than which nothing greater can be conceived'. He then asserted that it was greater to exist than not to exist. Therefore, he concluded, God must exist, for otherwise there would be something greater than God (namely whatever he had defined God to be plus the additional 'greater-making' quality of existence). Anselm appears to argue that merely understanding what is meant by the word God makes it clear that God exists.

Anselm's argument is discussed further later in this book. I wish to make clear at this point that this kind of proof that God exists is not required in order to make the case for theism. Were such a proof to be successfully produced, moreover — in other words if Anselm were shown to be right — then from our point of view such a success would undermine faith rather than establish it.

If what Pascal, Butler, Newman and Browning say is true, then there will always be a degree of uncertainty about whether God exists that reflects an absence of proof. At the same time, however, there must be evidence sufficient to make belief in God an act of commitment representing risk but not foolish defiance of reality. There must be more evidence than some existentialists desire for their 'splendid' leap of faith, but there may be less than Copleston required for his certain assurance of God's existence.

A final linguistic observation can make my position clear. There is a common tendency to distinguish between 'belief in' and 'belief that'. Belief in, we are told, implies an act of will, a decision to trust — as in 'I believe in you'. Belief that, on the other hand, is understood to be an acceptance of fact, and observation of what is the case — as in 'I believe that it is raining'. But it is clear that in the case of God both ingredients are required — an act of trust and factual observation. We do at times use 'belief in' language to mean something similar to 'belief that' — as in 'I believe in ghosts', which surely includes the idea, 'I believe that there is some evidence ghosts exist'. My view is that the religious believer who makes a credal statement such as 'I believe in God' is affirming something similar to the believer in ghosts. He or she is certainly making a commitment to trust God. But at the same time a claim is being made concerning factual evidence about God's existence. I would expect someone who claimed to believe in ghosts to give some evidence for their existence, and it is reasonable to expect the theist to give evidence for God's existence. But I do not consider it reasonable to expect the theist to prove the existence of God, something that would effectively remove the element of trust which I have also highlighted. The task of the theist, as I see it in this book, is to define what he or she means by the word 'God', and to give some evidence for believing that this Deity exists. Beyond that, however, it is not necessary for the theist to prove God's existence.

In *Language, Truth and Logic,* Ayer makes the following point about his religious position:

> It is important not to confuse this view of religious assertions with the view that is adopted by atheists or agnostics. For it is characteristic of an agnostic to hold that the existence of a god is a possibility in which there is no good reason either to believe or disbelieve; and it is characteristic of an atheist to hold that it is at least probable that no god exists.

We have seen already that Ayer identifies his position of 'no meaning atheism' as clearly distinct from both these positions.

What I have tried to set out in the last few pages is an understanding of 'meaning theism' which embraces a rather larger area than Ayer allows for. Pascal, for instance, held that it is 'at least probable that no god exists', and yet he chose to believe (in his terms of belief as a wager). Butler, Newman and Blougram might be considered agnostics according to Ayer's definition, or they might be considered theists. It would depend upon what Ayer meant by 'a good reason to believe or disbelieve'. The truth is that within the spectrum covered by 'meaning theism' and 'meaning atheism' there is no firm boundary marking the point where theism ends and agnosticism begins, or where agnosticism ends and atheism begins. Decisions are made on the basis of evidence, but they may be reversed. There is an obvious mixture of pointers both for and against the existence of a Deity. Conflicting interpretations compete for plausibility, and neither side can prove to the other its irrefutable correctness. We are in a state of perplexity. It may represent humanity coming to terms with a godless world. Or it may represent the God-given confusion which represents the opportunity for maturity outside the safe confines of the Garden of Eden. It is certainly tempting to say both to 'no meaning' atheists and to 'no meaning' theists that such perplexity represents the real life situation of most human beings as they choose to believe or not to believe in the existence of God.

philosophy and theology on common ground
In the course of this chapter I have taken an historical perspective upon the nature of religious belief, looking in particular at writers from the seventeenth to nineteenth centuries. But where is Christianity now in relation to questions of belief and the meaning of theism? How does this particular religious tradition shape up at the end of the twentieth century, particularly in the context of those challenges that it has faced over the last hundred and fifty years from movements in secular thought like Darwinism, Marxism and Positivism?

The example of Barth which we examined in the first chapter is one form of reaction. The intellectual challenge to Christianity in Western Europe and America over the last two hundred years has all too often tempted it to retreat into a ghetto ring-fenced by claims about the unassailable insights granted to those with faith. Yet Christianity is a religion that has always been open to rational criticism when its critics have been granted the freedom to make their challenge known. In the ancient Roman Empire, before Christianity acquired sufficient political power through the conversion of Constantine to enforce acceptance of its doctrines as a religious and political duty, there were many pagan critics who doubted, attacked and mocked its claims. Those doubts and attacks have been allowed to return in the modern era following the dissolution of theocratic ideas that have supposed a particular religious belief to be an essential ingredient of sound political organisation. But Christianity had so forgotten an earlier period when it was open to discussion and even mockery of its views that it reacted to the modern onslaught with what often amounted to fear and paranoia.

Despite the political reasons for their intellectual difficulties, many Christians persist in blaming only 'new ideas' rather than new political freedoms for increasing secularisation. They therefore adopt a deeply hostile stance towards intellectual developments of the last two hundred years such as Darwinism and Biblical Criticism, when they would have done better to engage with them and even turn them to their advantage. The ghetto mentality adopted by many Christians gives justice to the harsh comment made by Rubem Alves in a recent book, *Protestantism and Repression:* 'Doubt is the terror that has to be forgotten'. This may seem only to be valid comment upon a fundamentalist 'wing' of Christianity. But it goes further than that. Deeply woven into a number of academic approaches to the Christian religion is the psychological terror of doubt.

Take the case of Biblical Criticism. By any account this has offered a golden opportunity to understand the origins of Christianity more fully, to appreciate the social, economic, religious and political circumstances within which a Galilean Jew might impact so strongly upon world history.

But the opportunities have only been adopted half-heartedly. Many Christians started to worry that Christian faith was being made to rest upon the merely provisional conclusions of historians. Theologians pointed to what was dubbed the 'ugly broad ditch' of A.D. Lessing, namely that 'accidental truths' of history cannot be the basis of 'necessary truths of reason'. The beliefs of Christians could not, it was said, rest upon historical judgments, because these beliefs as 'truths of reason' would then depend upon the truths of history, which were only 'accidental' (in other words, they might not be the case). A conclusion is only as strong as its premises. If the premises might not be true, then the conclusion also might not be true.

The presumption is that the beliefs of Christians must be 'necessary truths' (beliefs whose falsehood is inconceivable). For this reason a number of theologians, right up to the modern day, have been profoundly uninterested in the historical debate over Christian origins. They have decided that the 'Jesus of history' is too elusive a being to provide a sure foundation for the 'Christ of faith'. They have turned towards an inner contact with Christ based upon faith which has sought to bypass the historical research that sought to determine, with an accuracy previous centuries could never manage, the nature of Jesus of Nazareth. As Martin Kähler put it a century ago in his tellingly-named book *The So-Called Historical Jesus and the Christ of Faith:* 'Christian faith and a history of Jesus repel each other like oil and water'.

Less than fifty years ago the German theologian Rudolf Bultmann, still the staple diet of theology undergraduates, declared in an essay entitled 'The Crisis of Belief':

> In the Christian message...there is absolutely no question of man's being given an historical account of a section of the past, which he might put to the test, or critically confirm or reject.

The result has been that a century which has seen so much development in terms of resources and method in historical research, has also seen a recurrent historical scepticism in theology. Many theologians have embraced a scepticism about the historicity of events or sayings in the life of Jesus which ancient historians have regarded as excessive when measured against their own assessments of other, secular figures in the past. The theologians' determination to rest their faith on something more secure than history has made them more than willing, in many circumstances, to accept that the historical evidence of Jesus' life is as patchy as the most sceptical secular historian

says it is. Their position is summed up by the Anglican theologian John Knox in his *Humanity and Divinity of Christ.*

> Since even the best attested fact of the history of the past can
> possess no more than a very high degree of probability and since,
> by definition, Christian and indeed all religious faith must from
> the believer's point of view be absolutely certain and secure, can
> faith ever be said to depend upon an historical fact, no matter
> how well established? Faith must know its object in a way we
> cannot know an historical fact.

On this basis, theology effectively refuses any common ground
with history. Insisting that religious faith must be absolutely
certain and secure, it decides that history can never provide such
security and thereby loses interest in history altogether. Instead,
it asserts that religious belief must have a way of 'knowing its
object' that is entirely separate from the process of historical
reconstruction. It retreats into the ghetto and dismisses the work
of the historian as irrelevant to its needs.

Precisely the same has happened all too often in the relationship
between the theologian and the philosopher. Philosophy has effectively challenged what the theologian often persists in seeing
as the 'proofs' of God's existence which he or she must hang on
to in order to have an absolutely secure and certain faith. Philosophers must therefore be excluded in the way that historians have
been excluded. Faith must 'know its object' in a way that philosophical reason cannot. The mistaken view is that only 'no meaning
theism' can secure the future of Christianity. Theology must
somehow be playing on a different pitch, with revelation determining the rules and faith the outcome.

The question that needs to be asked is: Can recent developments
in philosophical criticism be seen to support religious belief in the
way that recent developments in historical criticism can be seen
to do? Should the theologian attempt to make use of philosophy
in the way that those who have not reacted against Biblical
Criticism over the last hundred and fifty years have learned to
make use of history? Two trends in philosophy suggest that this
might be so.

The first trend is the movement within the philosophy of
religion away from the Cartesian view that if God existed some
proof of His existence must be capable of being set out, in the way
that Descartes himself attempted to set it out. There is a greater

recognition among philosophers that belief in God's existence does not need to be justified in these terms, and that theologians themselves do not seek to provide such justification. Arguments for the existence of God are no longer required to conform to Euclidean standards of proof — any more than are modern scientific hypotheses.

The second trend is the movement in thought associated with the development of Wittgenstein's thought between the early period of his *Tractatus* and the later period of his *Philosophical Investigations*. That development entailed a recognition that the concentration upon language by the school of logical positivism, within which Ayer's dismissal of religious belief emerged, might not so much show up the meaninglessness of theology as elicit its own particular logic. Wittgenstein's thought appears to show a progression from concentrating upon language in order to exclude certain forms of thought — as in Ayer's exclusion of metaphysics — towards concentrating upon language in order to make sense of those different forms in a way that was sensitive to their particular nature. The idea of 'Meaning as use' associated with the later Wittgenstein was never meant to imply that if enough people used a certain expression it must be true. But it did mean that in order to understand a particular way of thinking — for instance that of the theist — it was necessary to pay careful attention to the way in which theists actually spoke. It meant that philosophy was listening to what theologians were saying — even though it reserved the right to reject the theologian's arguments. Such sensitivity deserved a similarly receptive response from theology.

It suggested that theology should no more retreat to a 'no meaning' theist position in the face of philosophy than in the face of history.

'meaning theism' and the Christian personality

This chapter has argued not only for the compatibility of faith with intellectual uncertainty, but even for the necessity of such uncertainty for faith. This puts theology in a much stronger position to accept the challenge posed by historians and philosophers. It should encourage a willingness to engage on common ground, where 'meaning' theist and 'meaning' atheist conduct an argument in which each understands the other and indeed may convert the other. The spectrum of conviction concerning God's existence may run through several degrees of probability. Of course, those who, like Bishop Blougram, find it possible to share and even sympathise with the intellectual misgivings of the unbeliever, do not easily waver in their understanding. For belief in God, they would argue, is a very practical matter which is not given up lightly, particularly if it brings out the best in the believer: 'Belief or unbelief / Bears upon life, determines its whole course...' This does not mean they have to argue that their belief will never be given up. An experience of tragedy might convince them that God is not good. An argument about theism might convince them that God does not exist. Such uncertainty they accept as the God-given climate within which they learn about life.

At the same time, they are constantly weighing evidence. If they seek to 'prove' the existence of God, it is in the original sense of 'test' or 'try' rather than in the modern sense of 'demonstrate in such a way as to convey certainty'. They know that faith must be reasonable. But they also know that it need not achieve the sort of certainty that leads theologians to drive wedges between faith and reason, or faith and history, in a desperate attempt to achieve a level of conviction that is impossible in what they see as a hostile rather than a mature scientific environment.

The desire for certainty they would interpret as a possessive attempt to deny the divinely-intended distance between God and creation. It produces the archetypal image of the Christian, afraid of life, always trying to climb back into the Garden of Eden, by creating a world of fantasy if necessary to inhabit at the expense of living in the real world. Whether it is the timidly smiling cleric having tea, the piously confident student talking about the way in which Jesus warms up his or her heart, or the aggressively confident know-all trying to recall the country to 'civilisation', it is a similar picture of inability to come to terms with the way in which most people in Western societies live. Having read about the way in which Adam and Eve were beguiled out of the garden, Christians settle for being innocent as doves and leave others to be wise as serpents.

The rest of this book will not produce more than a flawed account of some of the arguments that have been advanced both concerning the physical and moral nature of God (because even if a God existed, there is still the question of whether we should worship Him or rebel against Him). But then anyone who picked up a book entitled *Does God Exist?* hoping to come away with the answer is liable to be disappointed. This debate will continue to be the context in life of every person, including those committed to belief in God. It may be that there is no God — every theist should be able to say that. But at the same time, if there is a God, it is perfectly plausible to argue that He would desire the discussion of His existence to proceed in the argumentative, confused and doubting way in which it currently does. Some will weigh the evidence one way and some will weigh it another, but no one, having made a decision to believe in God, will be able to say that their assessment cannot change as the argument proceeds. If God's existence is only a probability, that invites an element of commitment in believing which is excluded by certainty. That commitment can waver or disappear if the arguments of the philosopher or the historian appear to destroy its rational basis.

What I have tried to show is that exposure to these arguments may represent the will of a God who often desires more of a risk and venture in the faith of His creatures than they are willing to undertake.

notes

Butler, Joseph (1692-1752) An early example of a controversial Bishop of Durham(!), Joseph Butler's ideas were seen in particular as a challenge to Wesley's (not unlike the way in which the present Bishop of Durham is seen as a challenge to contemporary evangelical ways of thinking). His thought is best conveyed through some of his published sermons, although his most important work, containing the idea of probability as the guide to life, is *The Analogy of Religion.*

Descartes, René (1596-1650) A philosopher of such significance as to give rise to a school of thought in his name, Cartesianism. His arguments for the existence of God developed the 'Ontological

Argument' of Anselm into the form which Kant criticised in the eighteenth century. Descartes above all other philosophers popularised the idea that God's existence could be 'proved' in the sense of demonstrated with a mathematical certainty.

Kierkegaard, Søren (1813-1855) A Danish philosopher often regarded as the founding father of the modern school of thought 'existentialism', although the influence of this wide-ranging and original thinker can also be found in the neo-orthodox theology of Karl Barth. Kierkegaard's relatively short life was largely confined to Copenhagen, where after many years as a student he wrote a series of unsystematic works on philosophy, theology and aesthetics.

Newman, John Henry (1801-1890) A foremost leader of the Oxford Movement within Anglicanism, Newman later converted to Roman Catholicism and was finally made a Cardinal before his death. Many of his writings concentrated upon themes in the history of doctrine, but he also wrote significant works on the philosophy of religion, including the early *University Sermons* and the later *Essay in Aid of a Grammar of Assent.*

Pascal, Blaise (1623-1662) A French theologian and mathematician, Pascal is most famous for his unfinished *Pensées* (*Thoughts*), in which, by means of brilliant, pungent remarks, he attempts a vindication of Christianity through a series of perceptive observations whose psychological insight and aphoristic style anticipate the approach of the brilliant atheist Nietzsche in the nineteenth century. The idea that Christianity can only do justice to its beliefs by means of apparent contradictions (the notion of 'paradox') owes more to Pascal than to any other religious thinker.

Wittgenstein, Ludwig (1890-1951) One of the most brilliant of twentieth-century philosophers, Wittgenstein was destined to be one of the most quoted and misquoted by theologians. He is seen as a philosopher who passed through logical positivism (which he largely created with his early work *Tractatus Logico-Philosophicus*) to a position more sympathetic towards religious language as outlined in his later *Philosophical Investigations.* In fact Wittgenstein's famous dictum concerning the meaning of a word lying in its use was never designed to mean that if enough people said something there must be something in it! Nevertheless, it is fair to say that he was far more conscious of the reductionist tendencies in logical positivism than were others who passed through this particular school of thought.

further reading

A.J. Ayer's *Language, Truth and Logic* is still a pertinent and readable work, more than half a century after its original publication. Later editions have a useful introduction written in 1946 by Ayer himself, in which he revises some of the points made ten years earlier in what he calls 'a young man's book'.

As a part-review of Ayer's arguments, an accessible account can be found in Frederick Ferré's *Language, Logic and God*. Another useful primer would be M.J. Charlesworth's *Philosophy of Religion: The Historic Approaches*. On the specific idea of metaphysics, W.H. Walsh's book of that title provides a rather more hopeful view of the subject than does Ayer. For analysing the way in which theological terms like 'faith', 'grace' and 'revelation' are used in order to undergird the 'meaning' theist position, and for a more general discussion of the issues, there is a useful collection edited by Basil Mitchell called *Faith and Logic*.

3: does what exist?

defining the problem

The previous two chapters have tried to argue that theists do not have to induce in others, or claim for themselves, the certainty that God exists. Uncertainty about whether God exists can be interpreted as a condition of, rather than the negation of, faith in God.

However, there is a different form of uncertainty that cannot possibly help the theist's case, and that is uncertainty about what is meant by talking about God. Whatever the uncertainty about whether God exists, the theist has a duty to be precise about what he or she means by 'God'.

Sometimes the search for a definition is straightforward. People arguing about whether black swans exist, for instance, do not need to spend much time agreeing first what a black swan is. But in many, if not most, cases of 'existence arguments', things are not so simple. Yet without a common definition of what is supposed to exist, people can argue at or around but never with one another.

To illustrate, I will take what might be thought to be an example posing relatively few problems — the case of the Loch Ness monster.

when is a monster not a monster?

Some people argue that everyone who claims to have seen or to have photographed this animal has been either drunk, deceived by a log or interested in promoting the Scottish tourist industry. On the other hand, many people are quite prepared to concede that some animal or group of animals has been seen in the loch. The issue is whether this animal can be identified as the 'monster'.

There is (to date) only one photograph of the creature. This serpentine-shaped animal has been studied carefully by experts, and the general consensus is that the picture reveals a row of playful otters. For this reason, arguments for the existence of the monster based upon visual evidence have met with a good deal of scepticism.

Another approach has been to consider how a monster or family of monsters, if they did indeed exist in the loch, might be able to survive in a freshwater environment. Could they obtain enough food to sustain themselves? Those who believe that they could point out that Loch Ness is very deep, and moreover that it may be connected by a series of subterranean passages with the sea. This would allow for the fulfilment of a monster's dietary needs.

The subterranean passage view offers a plausible account of how the monsters could feed, but unfortunately in doing so it destroys another theory about 'Nessie', which is that the animal is a relic of the dinosaur age, possibly a plesiosaur. The plesiosaur argument claims that the subterranean passages became blocked off over thousands of years, leaving a remnant of the past trapped in the loch, defying the process of evolution. In which case, it is impossible to see how the plesiosaurs could obtain sufficient quantities of food to survive.

The most credible explanation offered by those who support the existence of the monster is one assuming that the passages to the open sea have remained open. It argues that the animal is a whale or a basking shark which has lost its way or even come inland to die. This could explain the very rare sightings (a family of plesiosaurs, for instance, would surely be seen more often).

A log; otters; a basking shark; a whale; a plesiosaur — these are the various theories. But which of them, if any, would prove that the monster existed? Certainly not the log or the otters. Perhaps the plesiosaur. What about the basking shark or the whale? It would certainly be remarkable to think of an inland loch containing something so large. On the other hand, even this Scottish Moby Dick would not be the 'extinct' species rediscovered, which the plesiosaur theory suggests. It would not be in the serpentine shape in which local tradition and the folklore of sea monsters tend to cast the creature, nor would it be the individual guardian of the loch, the watery Cerberus, which some like to think of Nessie as being.

It is therefore possible to imagine two opposite reactions if it were to be shown conclusively that the creature was a whale. One reaction would be: 'There is a monster after all. It's been proven.' The other reaction would be: 'The monster theory has finally been debunked. It's only a whale.' And the issue would turn into one of defining when a monster was not a monster. The argument about whether the monster existed could not be settled without preliminary discussion about what in general a monster was.

If this is true in the case of Nessie, it is doubly true in the case of God. The argument about whether God exists cannot be settled without prior agreement as to who or what God is. And that is not at all easy. People say things about God that make the task of understanding what they mean very difficult — for instance when they describe God as indefinable. For this reason the history of discussion between theists and atheists about the existence of God has been characterised by a great deal of mutual misunderstanding.

For example, there is a famous story about a conversation between the Emperor Napoleon and the astronomer Laplace. Laplace was looking through his telescope, and Napoleon asked him if he could recognise the Deity through it. 'I have no need of that hypothesis,' the astronomer replied.

This story is commonly understood as an atheistic jibe against religion. However, most theists now would agree with Laplace. They would readily accept that an omnipresent divine being cannot be viewed through a telescope, however powerful, just as heaven is not a place which can be spied upon as though it were a distant planet. God is no divine monster whose existence can be sounded out by the aerial equivalent of the sophisticated underwater sonar equipment used to test for the presence of Nessie. You don't have to believe in God in order to practise astronomy or to understand how the movement of the planets is regulated, as might have been thought to be the case before Isaac Newton's time. The Laplace argument, many theists would conclude, simply disproves the existence of a God that theists don't believe in anyway.

Countless arguments about the existence of God proceed — or fail to proceed — in this way. Theists grow impatient with what they see as the reductionist behaviour of atheists, whom they accuse of disproving something the theists never claimed to believe in. The atheists, on the other hand, grow impatient with the way in which the God of the theists appears to be a master of disguises. If the atheist uncovers 'His' identity, then lo and behold the theists start saying that it isn't God after all. 'He' is somewhere else. It seems that the atheist can never disprove the existence of a God that theists admit to believing in. But one conclusion from that observation is that the theists themselves have no idea what they believe in.

I shall begin, then, by trying to set out what it is that theists believe in and atheists don't. I shall try to answer the question: 'What is God?' before I set about trying to answer the question of whether or not this God exists.

many religions, many gods?

Given that Britain (like many other countries) is now recognisably a multi-faith society, it should be clear that we cannot conduct this enquiry from within the terms of Christianity alone. Excluding the interesting view of God offered by the various sects, there are apparently different forms of theism promoted by Jews, Christians, Moslems, Sikhs, Hindus and perhaps Buddhists in Britain alone. This reminds us that when talking in terms of 'theists' and 'atheists' we often forget that there are various kinds of theism.

It is all too easy to think in terms of 'theist versus atheist', when in fact the argument is one of 'theist versus theist'. The story of the martyrdom of Polycarp, the Christian Bishop of Smyrna in Asia Minor during the early second century A.D., illustrates this well. Polycarp is taken into the arena for the sort of gruesome death which some feel kept Christianity alive in its early period, and which certainly kept the Hollywood epic alive in the modern period. The Proconsul offers him a last-minute reprieve, however, if he will repent and swear by the genius of Caesar. The Proconsul commands him: 'Say: Away with the atheists'.

To this Roman official, it is the Christians who are the atheists. For they deny the existence of the pagan gods, of whom the

Emperor was one (so that they were guilty of treason as well as irreverence by refusing to acknowledge them). The Proconsul is not interested in the fact that Polycarp believes in the existence of another god. He is concerned only that the bishop denies the existence of those gods who were regarded as being essential protectors of the Roman Empire. Such a denial makes him an atheist like other Christians.

In response, however, Polycarp turns to the crowd in the amphitheatre and shouts out the words which the Proconsul has invited him to repeat as if they applied to the audience in the arena. 'Away with the atheists', he cries out, not as if the words applied to Christians but as if they applied to pagans. Needless to say, the response guaranteed his death. But it illustrated that Christians and pagans had similar views of each other. Pagans were as much atheists to Christians as Christians were atheists to pagans. Polycarp was no more interested in the pagan gods than the Proconsul was interested in the Christian God. Each side condemned the other as 'atheist', whilst firmly claiming to believe in a god or gods.

Fortunately, there is a more tolerant attitude towards other religions in most parts of the world today. Increased possibilities of travel together with the effects of immigration have also made possible a wider knowledge of the world's religious traditions. But the reality of many different forms of theism makes the answer to the question 'Does God exist?' more complicated. Which god or gods are we talking about? Do the different religions believe in the same god in different ways, or do they believe in different gods? Do some of them believe in gods that exist and others believe in gods that don't exist? Is our answer to the question 'Does God exist?' going to be: 'It depends which god'?

Some religious traditions, it needs to be remembered, do not believe in any god. This is sometimes said of Buddhism, but it would be more accurate to say that the question of God's existence is a debate within Buddhism itself, and that the different forms of Buddhism are partially the product of different answers to the question of God's existence.

Most religious traditions, however, do claim to be theistic — to believe in a god or gods. But do they believe in the same god or do they believe in different gods?

One popular religious writer who thinks that they believe in the same god is John Hick. His interpretation of the different forms of theism is well captured by the title of a book he wrote, called *God has Many Names*. If this was so, then 'Yahweh', 'God the Father' and 'Allah' would all refer to the same God, in the way that 'The President', 'George Bush' and 'Commander in Chief of the Armed Forces' all refer to the same person.

Hick once compared the different religious traditions to different planets in a solar system like our own, all of which orbit the same sun. They therefore represent a variety of approaches to the same god. In another analogy, he compared the religions to different paths towards the peak of a mountain, or different perspectives upon the same building. All these images make the claim that there is one God who is understood in a variety of ways by the world's different religious traditions.

Understandably, this presumption has come in for a great deal of criticism. I have already mentioned the fact that some religious traditions would deny (or at least dispute) the fact that they are theistic at all. There is also the question, which we shall look at more closely later in the chapter, of whether they all believe in only one god, that is to say: Are they all monotheistic? If not, Hick's position would presumably have to be that the many gods of one tradition were equivalent to the one god of another tradition. Moreover, there is a feeling that Hick's perspective is in danger of appearing patronising. Is it really any better to be saying to another religious tradition what John Hick presumably says, namely: 'Your God is really my God', than to be saying with Polycarp and the Proconsul: 'Your God doesn't exist'?

The existence of many faiths, and the belief in many different gods, makes the task of finding a definition of 'God' doubly difficult. It is as if the loch has filled up with many different monsters, each in turn requiring consideration of its claims to be Nessie. Whilst I cannot within the scope of a short book consider what each religion in turn has to say about God, I can at least take note of the religious pluralism of our time. I shall certainly go beyond the Judaeo-Christian tradition in examining the claims of theism. However, whilst I remain suspicious of Hick's cosy position, it may be possible to accept that there is something approaching a common theistic structure among a number of the world's religious traditions.

breaking down the stereotypes

We shall only consider a small number of the world's religions. They are sometimes referred to as the 'major' religious traditions, but this would be as misleading as referring to the other religions as 'primitive'. We have chosen the traditions which most Western students of religion learn about — Judaism, Christianity, Islam, Hinduism and Buddhism. We limit our comments to these only because some sort of limitation is inevitable, and not because these are somehow the 'important' ones.

Books on these five traditions commonly divide them into two major categories. In the first category are those often described as 'Western', although strictly speaking they are Near Eastern religions. They are Judaism, Christianity and Islam. They follow a common scriptural tradition, Christians seeing what they call the Old Testament fulfilled in the New Testament, and Islam seeing both fulfilled in the Qur'an. They all therefore talk about characters like Moses and Abraham, and Islam talks about characters in the Christian gospels like Jesus and Mary.

These three religions are associated with a common form of theism. They share a belief in one God, who created and sustains the world. They agree that this god is 'transcendent', that is to say separate from the universe which He brought into being. They address God in personal terms, using imagery drawn from human and animal life. In the Old Testament or Hebrew Bible, which is an important part of the sacred literature of all three religions, God is likened for instance to a judge, a king, a midwife and a mother eagle. In the New Testament, God is likened to a father, a shepherd and the owner of a vineyard (among other images, including some found in the Old Testament). In the Qur'an, which is the most sacred text of Moslems, God is more often described in terms of generalised epithets that we normally associate with human life — for instance, Hearer, Keeper, Guide and Pardoner. A number of these have been collected together by Moslems to constitute the ninety-nine 'most beautiful names' of God.

Because these three associated religions appear to have in common the belief in one transcendent personal creator, it is often assumed that they all believe in the same God. Their descriptions seem sufficiently close to one another to be taken as descriptions of the same divine being.

The second category of religions is associated with the East. In origin they are Indian traditions, Hinduism and (what is to some extent its off-shoot) Buddhism. These traditions are not readily associated with the same God as those of Near Eastern origin. Some forms of Buddhism appear to deny belief in the existence of any god, whilst Hinduism is often associated with belief in several gods (polytheism). Moreover these gods are said to be more part of the world's spiritual furniture than transcendent of it — perhaps more like the saints in Catholic tradition.

It is also said that Hinduism believes in an impersonal rather than a personal Deity. In the case of the Near Eastern traditions I talked of images which compared God to a guide or shepherd or mother eagle or father, all of them personal (or at least animate) metaphors. Characteristic of Hinduism, we are often told, is the sort of analogy which suggests that God permeates the world in the way that salt permeates water when mixed with it (this comparison appears in The Upanishads, a series of early Hindu sacred texts). Such an analogy suggests that the ultimate reality is an impersonal entity rather than a personal being. This, then, is often said to be another difference between the Near Eastern and the Indian traditions.

Because of maintaining an apparently different brand of theism, Hinduism is often viewed by those whose main contact is with the Near Eastern religions either as atheist or as believing in a different god or gods. In terms of the analogies we have used so far, the Indian traditions are said to orbit around a different sun, or to be climbing a different mountain — or to identify with a family of monsters in the loch quite different from the one followed by the Near Eastern religions.

It may be useful at this point simply to list the three main differences between the Near Eastern and the Indian religious traditions as they are often presented. Because of the pressure of space, I cannot enter into the arguments about whether Buddhism is a theistic religion, and how far it has moved away from its Hindu parent religion. I shall therefore concentrate upon Hinduism.

Near Eastern	*Indian (Hinduism)*
Monotheist (one god)	Polytheist (many gods)
God separate from world	God(s) in the world
Personal God	Impersonal God

A closer examination of the traditions, however, throws a question mark against these easy distinctions between the religious traditions of the Near East and India. I shall therefore look more closely at their teachings, partly because of the ecumenical value of an awareness of their doctrine, but mainly because we can thereby focus much more clearly upon what religions mean by 'God'.

I shall consider each of these apparent differences between the Near Eastern and Indian religious traditions in turn, beginning from the issue of polytheism and monotheism.

one God or many?

The following quotations are taken from the Hebrew Bible (what Christians call the 'Old Testament'), the New Testament, the Qur'an and the *Bhagavad Gita* (a Hindu sacred text):

Invoke no other god with Allah.

('The Story', 'sura' or chapter 28 of the Qur'an)

I am the Lord your God, who led you out of the Land of Egypt, out of the house of bondage. You shall have no other gods before me.

(Exodus 20:30)

Jesus answered, 'The first [commandment] is, "Hear, O Israel: the Lord our God, the Lord is One; and you shall love the Lord your God with all your heart, and with all your soul, and with all your mind, and with all your strength."'

(Mark 12:30)

If any worshipper do reverence with faith to any God whatever, I make his faith firm, And in that faith he reverences his God and gains his desires, For it is I who bestow them.

(*Bhagavad Gita* 7:21-22)

The first three quotations, from the Near Eastern religious traditions of Islam, Judaism, and Christianity, demand belief in only one god. But Christianity is the only religion that makes it clear that only one god exists. Therefore Judaism and Islam could be said to be in one sense polytheistic and in one sense monotheistic. They are polytheistic in that they seem to believe that many gods exist, but monotheistic in that they command obedience to only one of these many gods.

The quotation from the *Bhagavad Gita*, on the other hand, appears not only to recognise the existence of many gods but also to support the worship of many gods. It might, therefore, be said that if this is a fair representation of Hinduism, the major religion of the Far East, then Hinduism is polytheistic in two ways — both in saying that many gods exist and in saying that many gods may be followed.

It may seem as though Christianity is the most monotheistic religion. Not only does it command the following of only one god, but it also makes it clear that only one god exists. However, closer examination of the Christian religion puts a question mark against this. Christianity, unlike Judaism and Islam, talks about God as a 'Trinity'. God is Father, Son and Spirit, who together form 'one substance' according to the Christian creeds. Many Jews and Moslems have accused Christians of being in reality polytheists, arguing that the Christian Trinity in reality represents a belief in three gods rather than one. Indeed, in some ways the Christian idea that the three parts of the Trinity form together one underlying substance is closer to the Hindu understanding of one reality behind the many gods. The Christian idea of God as Trinity could be regarded as a bridge between the traditions of the Near East and the Far East.

I will not attempt here to develop further the complicated arguments about God as Trinity. My aim is only to point out that the situation is more complex than a simple division between 'Western monotheism' and 'Eastern polytheism'.

For instance, take the case of Judaism and Islam. Certainly they talk of other gods, but the nature of these gods is so different from that of the god whom Jews and Moslems are to follow that we might be tempted to deny that these others are gods at all. We are at once in the realm of 'when is a monster not a monster?' Just what does something have to be for it to be called a god?

For instance, take the following quotations from the Qur'an about Allah.

Praise be to Allah, the Creator of heaven and and earth!

There is nothing in heaven or earth beyond the power of Allah.
(Both from 'The Creator', sura 35)

These 'god-like' qualities cannot really belong to more than one being. If nothing in heaven or earth is 'beyond the power of Allah' — if Allah, in other words, is omnipotent — then this quality can only be attributed to Him and to no-one else. There cannot be another omnipotent god, in the way that there cannot be two monarchs or two presidents or two tallest men.

Allah is also unique in being the Creator. Just as everything is under His power, so everything derives from Him. As Creator He began it all; as all-powerful He sustains it all; as judge of the world He will complete it all and bring it to its consummation. These characteristics can only be true of one Deity.

We might compare what Moslems and Jews say about gods to what a very different tradition from the Mediterranean world says. The classical legends set down by ancient Greek poets like Homer referred to a number of gods, under their leader Zeus, supposedly located on Mount Olympus, who made occasional forays onto the human scene in various human or animal disguises. These stories describe a form of religion commonly described as paganism, and represent what can clearly be understood as a type of polytheism. The many gods are all of roughly equal power. None is in complete control of the world. None could be held up as creator, sustainer or judge of the world. They are more powerful actors on the stage than the human ones, but they neither built the set nor determine the play. Many people would refer to them more as superhuman than as divine characters. They are not so much gods as supermen and superwomen — more basking shark than Cerberus, to return to our Loch Ness analogy.

Although Judaism and Islam, like paganism, recognise in at least some of their sacred literature the existence of many gods, the gods in these religions are not all of equal power. One, the one they choose to worship, is so much more powerful than all the others that He belongs to what is in effect a different category of being. Indeed, it could well be argued that He alone truly fits the description 'God'. The rest are more like the pagan gods — supermen and superwomen. Perhaps for this reason Judaism and Islam, particularly when they refer to the creative power of the god whom they follow, suggest that their deity is in fact the only god who exists and not simply the only god who is to be worshipped:

> Men, bear in mind Allah's goodness towards you. Is there any other Creator who provides for you from heaven and earth? There is no God but Him. How then can you turn away from Him.
>
> (sura 35)

> For thus says the Lord,
> who created the heavens
> (He is God!)
> who formed the earth and made it
> (He established it;
> He did not create a chaos,
> He formed it to be inhabited!):
> 'I am the Lord and there is no other'.
>
> (Isaiah 45:18)

Judaism and Islam could be called polytheistic religions in the sense that they do contain traditions that represent Jews and Moslems as called upon to choose one of several gods and follow Him to the exclusion of others. The God of Judaism, for instance, reminds Israel in the book of Exodus when He gives Moses the Ten Commandments that He is a jealous God. Presumably, then, there is something for Him to be jealous of!

However, when we look closely at what is said about these various gods, we find that the god chosen by (or who chooses) Israel is quite unlike all the others. He is not one among equals. The question that must ultimately be asked about Israel's God is: 'Is there a God besides Me?' (Isaiah 44:8).

There are passages of the Bible which are compatible with polytheism. Take this quotation from Exodus 15:11:

> Who is like thee, O Lord, among the gods?
> Who is like thee, majestic in holiness,
> terrible in glorious deeds, doing wonders?

The Exodus narrative, identifying the God of Israel as the worker of wonders such as those which led Pharoah to release the Israelites from Egypt, could easily be thought of as referring to one god among many. The text asks, 'Who is like thee?', but what distinguishes this god — glorious deeds and wonders — is quite compatible with the existence of other gods performing glorious deeds and wonders of their own. Israel's God would be unique only in the sense that each of the gods on Mount Olympus is unique, with a particular history of actions and involvement in the human world.

By the time that the Book of Isaiah was written, however, things were being said about Israel's God that could not be said of any other, and this led increasingly to the claim that the God of Israel is the only one that exists. There can only be one Creator, one God who made the earth and maintains it under divine control. The other gods are mere pretenders to divinity. Not only is no other god like Israel's God: no other god *exists* (Isaiah 45:9).

In the course of its history Judaism developed its concept of God. The initial idea of God as the one who led the people 'out of the house of bondage', who freed the Israelite slaves from Egyptian control, develops into an idea of God as one who made the heavens and the earth. The notion of God as liberator was compatible with the existence of other gods. The notion of God as Creator was not. Whether this is seen as a straightforward historical progression from polytheism to monotheism, or whether it is seen more as bringing out ideas implicit in the Jewish religion from the beginning, there is a clear case for identifying Judaism as a monotheistic religion despite its limited recognition of other gods.

The existence of other gods who turn out to be mere 'pretenders' to divinity raises the question of what makes a god a God. Why are these other gods ultimately denied the status of true Deity? Why is only Israel's God allowed in the end to be a 'real' god? The answer seems to lie with the power of God. There can only be one supreme being responsible for managing the world. Only one God can have brought the world into being, supervise it in the present and bring it to its end. This appears to be a fundamental belief of Judaism and Islam. Christianity, however, does seem to envisage a degree of divine power-sharing among the persons of the Trinity. Since the Eastern traditions think very much in terms of a single divine power being shared out among many gods, the Christian doctrine of the Trinity could be viewed as a link between this view and the more familiar view of the 'Western monotheistic' traditions.

Let us turn to the major Eastern tradition, Hinduism. The quotation on page 53 from the *Bhagavad Gita* appears to support the idea not only that many gods exist but that many gods can be followed and worshipped. Does this not constitute a radically different form of theism from that practised by the Near Eastern religions?

However, although frequently described as polytheistic, it would be more accurate to describe Hinduism as a religion which has beome monotheistic by another route to that taken by the Near Eastern religions. Where the latter have rejected other gods in favour of the one they wish to follow, the former has attempted to assimilate the many gods in which it believes into a single Deity who stands behind them as their ground. In other words, for Hinduism the road to monotheism has been by way of syncretism (blending together) rather than rejection.

The passage from the *Bhagavad Gita* reflects the outcome of the process of syncretism, namely the idea of some further absolute being behind the gods that are reverenced.

> If any worshipper do reverence with faith to any God whatever, I make his faith firm. And in that faith he reverences his God and gains his desires, For it is I who bestow them.
>
> (*Bhagavad Gita* 7:21-2)

The question is: Who is the 'I' who makes firm the faith of those who reverence any god? Who bestows upon the worshippers the 'gain' of their 'desires'? Is it not the case that there is one absolute being whose power is shared among the gods, much as in Christian tradition one divine power is shared out among Father, Son and Holy Spirit?

Another analogy drawn from comparison with the Christian tradition would be as follows. Is it any more accurate to call Hinduism polytheistic because of its talk of many gods than to call Roman Catholicism polytheistic on account of its talk of many saints? Just as the Catholic saints, who may well be associated with particular areas or objects like Hindu gods, all manifest the same divine power, they can be reconciled with monotheism. Precisely the same can be said of the many divine beings reverenced from within Hindu tradition.

Such is the fluid nature of the Hindu syncretism that the unifying power behind the gods cannot be given a single name. The speaker in the quotation above is Krishna, but Krishna is himself described by other Hindu writings as a manifestation of the God Vishnu. What can be said, however, is that this sense of an ultimate monotheism according to which the gods are recognised to be manifestations of a single absolute reality is deeply woven into the religious tradition of Hindus. Whether it is said of Krishna or Vishnu or Siva, the same structure of religious thought recurs.

This must lead us to consider whether the differences in theistic belief between Near Eastern traditions like Judaism, Christianity, and Islam on the one hand, and Indian traditions like Hinduism on the other hand, have been exaggerated because of language. In Hinduism the manifestations of the highest reality are described as 'gods' rather than as 'angels' or 'powers'. This is unusual in the Near Eastern religions, although Christians sometimes talk of Jesus as 'God' (as in the words of Thomas after the Resurrection, 'My Lord and my God'— John 20:28), and in the doctrine of the Trinity it is made clear that the Father, the Son and the Spirit are all 'God' (as stated in the Athanasian Creed). However, it is all too easy for those brought up in the Near Eastern traditions, when they hear Hindus talking of many gods, to suppose that they are talking of what they consider to be the supreme reality. But this is not the case. There is a reality 'behind' these gods, and any account of the divine nature as Hindus conceive it to be must take this into account.

In the case of Judaism and Islam, we are led to question whether the 'other gods,' which Jews and Moslems are commanded to shun in favour of following Yahweh or Allah, are really gods at all. In the case of Hinduism, we are led to ask whether all the gods are really 'God', if by 'God' we intend to refer not to spiritual forces at work in the world but the absolute being who lies behind the gods themselves. We must not be misled by language. We may find works on Hinduism talking of a 'High God' and 'lesser gods', of 'demigods' and 'local divinities'. Whatever words are used, the tradition appears to be fundamentally monotheistic. The many gods do not share equal amounts of power. One stands behind the others as their overall ruler. In the Indian as in the Near Eastern traditions, the theistic structure is one which suggests the existence of a single supreme being, under whom many other divine forces may operate, but always at a lesser level to the one 'God' under whose control they ultimately stand.

I would conclude, then, that for all these traditions there is only one monster in the loch. Some Near Eastern religions demand allegiance to one of many monsters, but on closer examination it turns out that the other creatures in the loch are only large fish. There can be only one all-powerful creator and sustainer of the world. So far as Hinduism, the major Far Eastern religion, is concerned, there may be reference to many gods, but there is also a clear understanding that they are only large fish too, behind which lies a single, unifying absolute being, not unlike the one substance in three persons of the Christian Trinity. It is this being, the power behind the throne who acts as the unifying force of all the 'lesser' deities, who would more appropriately be described as *the* God of Hinduism.

in or out of the world?

The second supposed difference between the Near Eastern and the Indian religious traditions was that the former believe that God is separate from the world, whilst the latter make God or the gods a part of the world's spiritual furniture. In this area of discussion too there may be a closer theistic structure between the two religious groupings than we are often led to believe.

Take, for instance, the Near Eastern religions of Judaism, Christianity and Islam. These could be said to put their emphasis upon the 'transcendence' (separateness or otherness) of God. Indeed their sacred works contain passages that state bluntly that God is completely beyond our understanding and completely unlike anything which we know on earth.

Nevertheless, each of these traditions at the same time lays emphasis upon the 'immanence' (presence) of God in the world. The case of Islam provides an interesting example, because Islam is commonly regarded as the most strictly monotheistic of the Near Eastern religions. That is to say, it believes in one God and distances that God completely from the world as utterly transcendent. It attacks Christianity for its doctrine of the Incarnation, which is seen to suggest that God could be a human being. Worshipping

Jesus as 'Lord' is taken to imply identifying Jesus as God. Even the way in which Jews called their religious teachers 'rabbis' is suspected of applying some form of divinity to them. Islam, it is said, is the religion most concerned to prevent any identification of the divine with what is earthly and human. Mohammed is seen as someone who swept away the pagan polytheism of Mecca in favour of the idea that there is one God who is totally separate from the world. An examination of the Qur'an, however, reveals that despite the traditional association of Islam with emphasis upon the transcendence of God, it also highlights the divine immanence or presence. In sura 50, we find a famous passage which reads:

> We created man. We know the promptings of his soul, and we are closer to him than the vein in his neck.

God may be totally other to humanity, but at the same time (as in the quotation from sura 50) God is said to be closer to a human being than is his or her jugular vein.

In sura 24, the Qur'an declares that 'Allah is the light of the heavens and the earth'. Light is often used as a metaphor for God because it can convey both the presence and the unapproachability of the divine being. It can convey unapproachability, because a dazzling light turns away those who seek to gaze at it directly. On the other hand, it conveys God's presence because light shines down upon the world and illuminates everything within it.

In another sura (57), God is described as 'the visible [or manifest] and unseen'. Islam would never, of course, suggest that God was in any way a visible object. But it does make clear a belief that the divine being reveals or manifests its nature in the world. The God who is hidden to sight and beyond human understanding is also the God made manifest in our earthly environment.

This double emphasis upon the transcendence and the immanence of God can be recognised from the other Near Eastern religions. In a well-known Christian discourse, chapter 17 of The Acts of the Apostles, St Paul makes a speech to the Athenians in which he refers to an altar inscribed with the words, 'To an unknown God'. He goes on to say: 'What therefore you worship as unknown, this I proclaim to you' (Acts 17:23). About this God Paul says two things: on the one hand, 'He' is 'the God who made the world and everything in it', who 'does not live in shrines made by man' (17:24); on the other hand, 'He' is not far from each one of us, for 'in Him we live and move and have our being' (17:27-8). The first quotation affirms the transcendence of God, who is not part of the world's furniture, like an idol in a shrine. The second quotation affirms the presence of God, in whom we live and move and have our being — emphasis upon the closeness of God akin to the Islamic passage about God being nearer to us than our neck-veins.

From Jewish tradition we have a clear statement of God's inescapable presence:

If I ascend to heaven, thou are there!
If I make my bed in Sheol, thou art there!
If I take the wings of the morning and
dwell in the uttermost parts of the sea,
even there thy hand shall lead me,
and thy right hand shall hold me.

(Psalm139: 8-10)

When we recognise that for the three Near Eastern traditions there is a clear emphasis upon God's presence as well as His transcendence, their approach is seen to be closer than might be imagined to that of the Indian religious traditions.

A reading of some of the sacred texts of Hinduism and even non-theistic Buddhism arguably reveals a vision of reality permeated by a single transcendent being as clearly as do the texts and commentaries of the Near Eastern religions. In *The Upanishads* (Hindu sacred texts) God is described in the following terms:

He encircles all things, radiant and bodyless, unharmed, and untouched by evil.
All-seeing, all-wise, all-present, self-existent, He has made all things well for ever and ever.

In the *Bhagavad Gita*, Krishna speaks in the following terms of the divine being:

I am the dice-play of the gamester,
I am the glory of the glorious,
I am the victory, I am courage,
I am the goodness of the virtuous...
...and I am the seed of all that is born...

There is nothing that can exist without me.
There is no end to my holy powers...
And whatever is mighty or fortunate or strong
springs from a portion of my glory.

It is, of course, impossible to do justice to the thought of a
religious tradition with one or two quotations. But they are
enough, perhaps, to convey the fact that Hinduism is not a
pantheistic alternative to the Near Eastern or Western forms of
theism. There is a sense of God's transcendence in Hinduism
just as there is a sense of God's immanence in Judaism, Christianity and Islam. All these traditions attempt to represent the
way in which God both permeates and undergirds the universe
on the one hand, whilst transcending it on the other. Such a
concept clearly requires further exploration, which I attempt in
the next chapter. Nevertheless, it can be claimed that such
exploration will be discussing a theistic structure found in the
Eastern as well as the Western traditions.

He, She or It — a personal God?

I have already mentioned that the sacred literature of the Near
Eastern traditions contains many images of God as a person —
judge, king, father, guide, keeper, shepherd and so on. Recent
feminist commentaries have pointed out that these images of God
are not all of a male person. Female imagery of God is used
particularly in connection with creation, which is compared to a
woman giving birth. God's constant watch over the created world
is compared to that of a female bird caring for its young, or a
woman suckling her child (these images come from the Hebrew
Bible or Old Testament). There is also imagery of God as a woman
which is nothing to do with specific female roles such as giving
birth. In the New Testament Jesus uses two images to convey
God's extravagant concern for the world: one is the shepherd who
risks the rest of the flock in order to go searching for the lost sheep;
the other is the woman who turns a house upside down looking
for lost coins. God the Shepherd seems to have become well-es-
tablished within Christianity, but God the Housekeeper less so.
Nevertheless, they are given equal prominence in the New Testament, and should be given equal weight as images of God.

However, it is also clear that there are impersonal images of God in these traditions. In a famous passage from the Psalms, personal and impersonal images run side by side:

I love thee, O Lord, my strength.
The Lord is my rock, and my fortress,
and my deliverer,
my God, my rock, in whom I take refuge,
my shield, and the horn of my salvation,
my stronghold....

(Psalm 18: 1-2).

I have already referred to the passage of the Qur'an where God is described as 'the light of the heaven and the earth'. To suppose that the divine being is always represented by the Near Eastern religions in terms of personal (or at least animate) imagery would be a mistake.

A similar mistake would be the supposition that Indian religious traditions always represent God in terms of impersonal imagery. I have mentioned one example of such imagery already — the comparison between God's relation to the world and salt dissolving in water. Such imagery is comparable to the idea of light diffused throughout the world. Moreover, it is combined with a great deal of personal imagery in many Indian religious traditions. One example comes from the *Sivananasiddhiyar,* the most important sacred text of a form of Hinduism common among the Tamils of Southern India, Saivism:

Whatever god you accept, he [Siva] is that god.
Other gods die and are born, and suffer and sin.
They cannot reward,
But he will see and reward your worship.

We see here the familiar Hindu approach of assimilating many gods into one underlying Deity rather than rejecting some gods in favour of others. What we also see is a description of this underlying God which can only make sense in personal terms. Impersonal entities cannot overlook and reward worshippers.

The truth is that in both Near Eastern and Indian religious traditions there is a combination of personal and impersonal imagery in describing God, just as there is a combination of emphasis upon both the transcendence and the immanence of the divine being.

a common theistic structure

This chapter leaves crucial questions unasked, such as: What sense does it make to talk of a God who is both 'in' and 'out' of the world? How can God be both personal and impersonal? I shall attempt to look at these issues in the next chapter. What I have tried to do here is to suggest, without wanting to be closely associated with Hick's pseudo-ecumenical approach, that among many of the world's religions there may be a common understanding of the divine nature. Behind the differences — which are often more of language and emphasis than of substance — there may be a common view that God is One, present in the world and yet transcending it, personal lord or saviour or protector and yet impersonal reality.

But is this a common definition among several religions or a common confusion? Is this view of the divine nature not totally meaningless? I shall try to unravel some meaning in my next chapter.

notes

The *Bhagavad Gita* Regarded as one of the finest religious poems in the world, the *Bhagavad Gita* forms one of the most important sacred texts of Hinduism. Along with the sermon on the Mount, it was the favourite reading of Mahatma Gandhi and indeed both (in very different ways) encourage selfless devotion to others and the principle that the end does not justify the means.

The Qur'an (or Koran) The Islamic scriptures, divided into one hundred and fourteen 'suras' or chapters. The first edition was produced some twenty years after the death of Mohammed — a much smaller gap than that between the death of Jesus and the emergence of the New Testament! It is held by Moslems to contain all the essentials of their belief, and to be a collection of passages of direct revelation uttered by Mohammed (although not all written down during his lifetime). When the verses of the Qur'an are quoted a Moslem begins: 'God has said'. Mohammed's role is seen as entirely passive, passing on what God has told him. By comparison, Jews and Christians have a much stronger sense of human involvement in the writing of the Bible.

further reading

One of the most controversial religious works of the 1960s, John Robinson's *Honest to God*, is a well-written and clear introduction (from a Christian perspective) to the problem of defining what God is, and the difficulty of bringing together theological description, popular imagery and the language of worship.

John Hick's *God and the Universe of Faith* introduces the 'ecumenical' idea of many faiths believing in the same God. The problems with this assessment are briefly and clearly discussed in Brian Hebblethwaite's *The Problems of Theology*, chapter 2: 'Theology and Comparative Religion'. A good introduction to the multi-faith context within which theism should be discussed is Jean Holm's *The Study of Religions*.

An excellent short defence of female imagery for God is provided by *The Motherhood of God*, a report commissioned by the Church of Scotland and published by the St Andrew's Press.

4: the nature of God

introduction

Traditional approaches to the problem of defining God's nature
have often concentrated upon running through a list of divine
attributes and classifying them in various forms. For instance, a
common approach is to identify three ways of defining God,
known as the ways of 'eminence', 'analogy' and 'negation'. The
different characteristics of the Deity are then shown to reflect one
or other of these ways. For instance, the definition of God as
'infinite' is said to be an example of the way of negation. By
calling God infinite, we are denying Him a characteristic of
objects in the world. Adjectives like 'infinite', 'unchanging' or
'impassible' could be taken as simple denials that what characterises reality as we know it characterises God.

It is clear enough that nothing can be defined simply in negative
terms. Other divine attributes, however, appear to state positive
things about God. The so-called 'moral' attributes are often cited
in this context — ideas that God is wise, good, just, loving and so
on. We discuss the idea of goodness in the next chapter, but what
we can note here is that these characteristics have traditionally
been regarded as examples of the way of eminence — of God
possessing perfectly what we possess imperfectly. Thus it is
claimed that God is perfectly just, where we are imperfectly so —
indeed it is sometimes said that God is 'justice' or 'justice itself'.

However, it is not only the 'moral' as opposed to 'natural'
qualities that are treated in this way. Take, for instance, the
attribute 'omnipresence'. Is this an example of the way of negation
or the way of eminence? In a sense it is an example of the former.
It denies that God has particular location. But at the same time it

is surely doing more than assert what God is not. It is talking about an omni*presence* of God. It could equally be phrased in a way that fits in more with the way of eminence. In other words, it could be taken as saying that God's presence is universal and complete, ours is partial and incomplete. And what of the attribute 'eternal'? Does this mean that God is 'not in time' — an example of the way of negation — or does it, as some have said, mean that all times are somehow 'present' to God, in which case it might be claimed that God possesses a kind of temporal omnipresence?

Then take the case of the way of analogy. This has often been criticised because we are told that in drawing an analogy we normally know 'both sides' that we are comparing (eg 'doesn't he look like a horse?', where we can look at both and judge), whereas in this case we can only look at one side, the object that we are comparing with God. We cannot enter into this philosophical debate here, but what we should note — and what will be obvious to anyone soaked in the traditions of religion — is that all the world's religious faiths use endless analogies for God with promiscuous abandon. We have encountered them throughout the book. Mother, eagle, rock, father, keeper, guide, stronghold, nurse, housekeeper — the cynic might say: you name it, God's been compared to it!

What results from this is that we might be led to think that the problem with defining God is that there is a whole range of ideas about the divine being that tend to produce no very clear overall picture. We have a jigsaw puzzle with the pieces jumbled up.

For this reason I will not concentrate upon analysing or categorising lists of attributes. My approach is to make general observations about the structure of theism. I will concentrate upon two of the more difficult threads in the pattern I attempted to draw out in the last chapter, and will try to develop them further in a more philosophically coherent way. This chapter is, therefore, devoted to a discussion of God as transcendent yet immanent on the one hand, and as personal yet impersonal on the other.

transcendent and immanent?

What sort of a deity can be both separate from, and present within, the world? Is it a pure contradiction to affirm both these things at the same time? When the Qur'an talks of God as 'visible and unseen', or when the famous Christian theologian Dietrich Bonhoeffer defines God as 'the beyond in our midst', are they saying anything meaningful?

We can begin to answer this question by listing three principles concerning the divine which have emerged from the analysis in the previous chapter:

1   God is not an object or part of the world. God is not an idol in a shrine, nor the name of a spiritual force located in particular things like trees or stones. Nor is any holy person God, whether it be Moses or Jesus or Mohammed. None of the traditions asserts that. Even Christianity, which calls Jesus 'divine', makes clear that he prays to, depends upon, and is resurrected by a Deity whom he introduces to his disciples as God the Father.

2   God is not equivalent to the world. This point must be made in order to distinguish these religious traditions from a 'pantheist' position, which identifies God with nature. 'God' is not the name for everything that exists considered as a unity.

3   God is not an object outside the world, something you look 'beyond' in order to see. This is perhaps the most important point to make. After all, many popular images of God treat the Deity in this way. Take, for instance, the common idea of God as an old man on a cloud. Or take the many references to God as a being who looks down upon the world from some sort of celestial vantage point. This is, of course, precisely the divinity with which Napoleon teased Laplace. He challenged him to see God through his telescope. But this idea of God as an object up above the world (or up above the universe) is firmly ruled out by all that these religions have to say about the divine nature. The God believed in by Jews, Hindus and Christians, is not like the pagan God, Atlas, who was supposed to be underneath the world propping it up on his shoulders.

The third principle tells us that when we call God 'transcendent' we are not saying that God is 'above', 'outside' or 'beyond' the universe. Such language inevitably contradicts itself. It implies that there is a physical boundary to the universe, and that God exists 'outside' it much as the President of France exists 'outside' Britain. By saying that God 'transcends' the universe we are saying that none of the limitations that apply to finite life — such as being in a particular place — applies to God. When Paul denies that God is an idol in a shrine, he effectively denies that God is anywhere else too. As transcendent, God cannot be located, since location applies to what exists in the universe we know. A transcendent monster is not a monster who has escaped the loch and sits on a hill outside it.

It is all too easy for this principle to be forgotten. Believers then follow the practice of the person who stubs his foot on a stone and looks upwards with the cry, 'Oh God!' as if hoping for some sympathetic supernatural spectator to be looking down on what is happening. We have to remember that Napoleon and the literal believers in old men on clouds have got it wrong. God is not 'up there' — not on a cloud, not in an upstairs heaven and not waiting to be glimpsed through the end of Laplace's powerful telescope.

To think that God can be some further reality beyond the reality we know is simply to have failed to define the reality we know widely enough. It is to have failed to give the transcendence of God its proper cash value, to have weakened it so that it means something like 'outside the solar system' or 'above the galaxy'. The ghost of Laplace is hard to exorcise. But once we do so, once we see that by calling God 'transcendent' we are not banishing Him to some distant celestial isle from which to look down on us, then it becomes easier and not harder to understand His presence.

How does this understanding of God's transcendence clarify what it means to talk of the divine immanence or presence? It should be clear that a God who was simply 'outside' the world in the way that the President of France was 'outside' Britain could hardly at the same time be present in it. If 'transcendent' meant 'spatially removed' from us, and 'immanent' meant 'spatially present' among us, then it would be an obvious contradiction to say that God was both transcendent and immanent. But if 'transcendence' means not that God is physically distant from the world, but that none of the characteristics of finite human life, like location, duration and change, applies to Him, then it is at least not an obvious contradiction to call Him both 'transcendent' *and* 'immanent'.

It is important to be clear that the Deity does not lose its transcendence by being immanent. God is always *both* transcendent *and* immanent. Even Christianity, which is in danger of saying that when God 'became' man in Jesus He gave up all the attributes of divinity, like omnipresence, draws back from saying so, admitting that God 'put on' or 'added' humanity to His unchanging divinity during the Incarnation. Such a view presents Christians with particular problems in their idea of God (though also with benefits, examined more closely in chapter 6), but it demonstrates that they are consistent with the other traditions in what they say. When God is present, He does not cease to be transcendent.

What, then, does such 'immanence' mean? Just as the third principle, which rejected the idea that God is an object 'outside' the universe, clarified what we mean by 'transcendence', so the first principle clarifies what we mean by 'immanence'. God is not to be identified with what we have called a part of the world's furniture: God is no more an object inside the world than an object outside it.

We therefore have to know: what sort of presence could there be of a God to whom there applied none of the limitations that applied to finite human existence? This question has been answered by describing the nature of God in a number of ways. I shall examine two in this section — the comparison of God to light, and the understanding of God as existence:

(a) *Light*. The analogy to light has been a favourite religious image when talking of God. In a number of ways it has proved an attractive metaphor.

First, light is seen as something that permeates reality in its entirety. It is not limited to a particular place. Similarly, the argument goes, God's presence is an omnipresence: he is everywhere.

Second, when the question turns to *how* God is everywhere, the analogy to light is seen as useful. Imagine walking out one day and thinking about the light. You would not say that it was a part of anything around you — it does not attach itself to things or become a particular quality that they have. Light is not visible as an object in a particular place: rather, it operates as the invisible catalyst through which everything around takes form and shape. If we were to refer to the light, we would not associate it with an individual object. We would say: 'It is light', but would not refer to any particular thing by the 'It'. We might say that we were going out 'into the light', but here again the light would be the general environment within which we did everything else. It would not be itself a thing. Going into the light is not like going into the street.

The presence of God, like the presence of light, is seen as universal and enabling. As the quotation from the poets cited by St Paul has it: 'In Him we live and move and have our being.' It is also seen as similarly elusive, something in terms of which everything else has objectivity but which cannot itself be determined as an object.

(b) *Existence.* Whilst religious traditions may prefer the theme of light as more poetic, their theologians find more prosaic ways to represent the divine presence. One which has been thoroughly explored is that of 'being'. Philosophers of religion have considered what it means to say that something 'is'. They have thought of existence, in the way that others have thought of light, as something that permeates all things without becoming a part of them. They have been particularly interested in a fact that I touched upon earlier when discussing the 'Ontological Argument', namely that existence is not a quality or attribute of something in the way that being round, or hard, or long-haired is an attribute. They have therefore wondered what it means to say that something 'exists', when existence does not appear to attach any particular characteristic to it. Some of them have concluded that existence constitutes that universal and elusive divine presence which can never be pinned down as a particular constituent of reality. God, they have said, is 'being' or 'being itself' (by which they mean that all else has to be 'something', whereas God as pure being simply 'is'). To say that God is present in the world, they would argue, is to say that the world has existence.

This debate re-opens some of the issues that were touched upon in the first chapter concerning the nature of metaphysics and the argument that Ayer acts in a reductionist way by proscribing, in effect, certain interpretations of reality. According to Ayer, by mistaking existence as an attribute religious thinkers like Anselm had constructed an entirely bogus 'proof' of God's existence. Metaphysics was seen by Ayer as a product of linguistic confusion. It would become redundant as soon as the meaning of certain words was made clear.

But it may be, as this discussion suggests, that whilst the confusion Ayer points to is a real one, the meaning of the word 'existence' is genuinely complex. It is certainly the case that the idea that existence is not a predicate, a quality of things such as blueness or hardness, was clearly recognised in classical philosophy long before it was taken up by Kant in the eighteenth century and further refined by Bertrand Russell in the twentieth. Some philosophers of religion, particularly those in the Christian Thomist school (the school that follows the thought of Thomas Aquinas), would see in the idea of existence a key to representing the omnipresence of a transcendent God. They would say that by existing things reflect the presence in them of that which transcends them. And they would find this fact indicated by peculiarities in the use of the word 'being' or 'existence' which the logical positivist critique doesn't begin to take account of.

Obviously more questions are raised here than can possibly be answered in a short book. All I can try to do is to outline what theists have been saying when they talk of God, and to try to offset some popular misconceptions of what they mean. Although I have so far been concentrating on Thomist interpretations of existence, there have been equally profound examinations in Buddhist and Moslem tradition, and in the modern day by existentialist writers, some of whom are religious and some of whom are not.

The references I have made to light and existence only touch the surface of a very complicated debate. But by mentioning them I have perhaps been able to show that when theists talk of God as 'both far and near', or as 'visible and unseen', they are not guilty of a simple contradiction in terms.

To conclude this section, I would like to suggest that there is a common presumption among theists who explore, in their different ways, the nature of God as light or as existence. The presumption is that there is some inherent incompleteness or dependence about reality as we know it. This is arguably the fundamental point made by a famous set of attempted proofs of God's existence associated with the medieval theologian, Aquinas. These use arguments that have become familiar in the philosophy of religion. For instance, it is claimed that the world shows evidence of design or purpose: therefore, it is concluded that there must be a divine designer. Another common argument is to point out that everything in the world must have a cause, but that at the end of the line there must be an uncaused or 'first' cause.

As proofs of God's existence these arguments fail to convince many people. For example, would our designer or first cause, even if one existed, *have* to be God? Would there have to be *one* designer, or could not the world have been designed by several working together? On the other hand, there is a strong case to be made that Aquinas is not setting out to provide proofs of God's existence. He is trying to describe the way in which the world as finite is not self-sufficient.

Take, for instance, the argument about a first cause. As a suggestion that change in the world occurs rather in the way that certain competitions present dominoes falling into kaleidoscopic patterns, requiring some initial push in order to begin the process, this 'proof' is hardly convincing. But some commentators have insisted that this sort of analogy misunderstands what Aquinas is saying. He is not making a temporal point about something that must have happened 'in the beginning' — the first push. To represent the dependence of the world upon God it is a classic error to suggest that it is like a car that requires an initial shove down the street and thereafter runs of its own accord. The error is well-ingrained, however: in chapter 5 we look at another famous image of the world's relation to God coined by William Paley, that of a watch to a watchmaker. Yet again, the idea is that once created the watch is self-sufficient and requires no further help from its divine craftsperson. All these analogies present a picture of God setting the process up (creating), and then effectively sitting back and letting it continue of its own accord.

The form of dependence of the world upon God suggested by Aquinas, however, is arguably a continuous rather than an initial dependence. Once created, the world does not become self-sufficient. Indeed some theologians argue that 'creation' refers not to what happened 'in the beginning' but to a constant dependence of the world upon God. As Augustine pointed out, creation did not happen literally 'in the beginning' for it did not happen 'in' time: rather, time was itself a part of creation. The world is eternally dependent. A famous early Christian image compared the universe to a tune which at any moment the creator might choose to end with silence. Such an image, unlike Paley's comparison to a watch, makes clear the theist claim that the created universe can never be understood as self-supporting.

An analogy which would better express Aquinas' view compares the universe to a number of objects, say a pile of books on a table. Each book in the pile depends upon the one underneath it to hold it up. The whole pile depends upon the table. The table depends upon the floor for support. And so on. This is the sort of image that, some commentators argue, Aquinas is trying to convey. The dependence of the world upon God is not initial but constant; built into the structures of reality is an inherent dependence which requires us to posit something else — the designer or the first cause.

Theists who explore notions like existence in order to express the presence of a transcendent God presume this inherent incompleteness in reality. They believe that reality 'points beyond itself' in the sort of way that the pile of books points beyond itself, in that we know something must be holding it up or it would fall. If we had no possibility of observing directly what was holding it up, we could still argue that something must be there. Reality, theists would argue, has this character. It could not be what it is without that upon which it depends. However, we have no power directly to observe that upon which it depends. Such a power would mean a capacity to see God directly which they are careful to rule out. It would be like the attempt to look directly at the sun that dazzles and finally blinds rather than enlightens.

Theists describe a constant dependence of the world not upon something outside it — if we define the universe broadly enough nothing *can* be outside it —but upon something that transcends it. They attempt to point out ways in which the world bears its self-insufficiency in its fundamental constitution, as being what it is, as existing.

The argument of the theist concerning God as both transcendent and immanent can be summarised in the following question and answer form:

1 How is God known? God is known through our knowledge of the world. God is not an object outside the world.

2 How is God known through our knowledge of the world? God is known neither as a part of the world nor as identical with the world, but as that which transcends the world.

3 How is God known as that which transcends the world? God is that upon which the world depends. But it is not possible to look beyond the world in order to see what it depends upon directly. That would be like looking underneath the world to see Atlas'

shoulders holding it up. What the theist claims is that by observing the world as it is, not by attempting to look outside it, one can see that it bears within itself a fundamental self-insufficiency. If we observe a pile of books hanging in the air, we might say: 'They must be resting on something.' Theists argue that this is what they are drawn to say about the whole of reality. But whereas one can at least look underneath the books for evidence of something underneath them, one can never look 'outside' reality. It has to be possible to see within reality the presence of that which transcends it — what the Christian theologian Dietrich Bonhoeffer called 'the beyond in our midst'. This is what philosophers of religion have attempted to explore in their complex analyses of existence.

He, She or It — a personal God?

The second part of the theistic pattern sketched in the last chapter which we need to put under the microscope is that which described God both as personal and as impersonal. As with transcendence and immanence, this may at first sight appear to represent a flat contradiction in terms. How can we make some sense of it?

To begin with, we must draw a distinction between God as personal and God as a person. Clearly none of the religious traditions we have examined asserts the latter. A useful example here would be Christianity. This religion concentrates upon a particular person, Jesus of Nazareth, but in its definition of God it describes the divine being as a Trinity — that is to say three persons. Moreover, it is frequently pointed out that the early Christian definitions of faith did not mean by the Greek and Latin words that we commonly translate as 'person' exactly what we would mean by 'person' today. There is no room here for a highly technical debate about language, but what is clear is that Christianity cannot possibly associate any view of God with what we would normally conceive a person to be. Nor can we think of the Christian God as three persons in the way that we normally consider them to be, or we would surely have to conclude that it was a religion committed to polytheism. Christians recognise this, of course, and therefore they emphasise that their three divine persons form a unity as 'one substance'. I will not enter here into the complex Christian debate over the nature of the Trinity. What we can clearly recognise, however, is that it is a religion committed to a view that God is personal in a different manner from that in which individual human beings are personal.

Given that this is so, what sense can we make of the way in which God, as opposed to John or Jane Smith, is personal? What sense can be made of divine as opposed to human 'personality'?

Once we try to lift the imagination away from the idea of God as a person (another unfortunate implication of the old man on a cloud motif) into another form of personality, we encounter a number of interesting arguments. Clearly a great deal of what religious traditions have to say about the Deity presupposes a personal God. We think of a being who shows various emotions towards creation — love, wrath, anger, sorrow, mercy and so on — and who is associated with particular activities that we think of as actions taken by persons, such as judgement. But how can we combine these personal activities with the idea of God as salt or (as in the last section) light or existence, analogies which we apparently need when trying to make sense, for instance, of God's omnipresence?

Let us begin by considering why we want to think of God in personal terms at all. One reason advanced by some is that we tend to value the personal above other things. We treat persons with a respect denied to animals and objects. In the terms of the old philosophical dilemma, most of us would save the endangered baby from the house before we'd save the Mona Lisa — even if the baby were far more likely to grow up an art thief than another Michelangelo or Da Vinci! Calling God 'personal' is partly the product of a desire to associate with Him what we most value in ourselves and our environment.

But what is it, exactly, that we value in the personal? Why are people more attractive to us than sunsets, even though at times we'd rather escape the people for nature? In part, it seems that the reason lies in an idea of a 'scale of being'. There is a form of progress — not moral, but at least in complexity — from the inanimate to the animate, from plant to animal, from animal to human. Many philosophers have spoken of this progress, identifying key stages in it, for instance the achievement of consciousness by animals or self-consciousness by humans. The human appears as the culmination and highest point of this process on earth.

What characterises ascending stages of the scale of being is the combination of unity with ever increasing degrees of complexity. The individual plant has growth without movement. Animals possess growth, movement and a consciousness of what is not themselves. Humans possess not only this, but also a conscious-ness of themselves in relation to the world around them. Some philosophers of religion have seen God as a higher stage of this process. The doctrine of the Trinity perfectly describes, they feel, the highest unity containing the highest inner complexity, repre-sented by the idea of 'three persons in one substance'. That God is personal by being tri-personal, they would say, means that in God the activity which at the human level must be divided between separate individual selves can be contained at the divine level within one being. At the top of the scale of being, then, is the most complex unity of all: God.

Others might argue that this idea of the personal as a form of unity admitting the most internal complexity is beside the point. They would highlight certain characteristics of human beings, such as emotions or the capacity to make moral choices, as characteristics that they wish to value above all others. They naturally, therefore, think of God as possessing what they value most in themselves. For the Christian, it is natural that God should become a person at the Incarnation rather than a dog or a stone, not necessarily because persons are somehow more technically advanced on a scale of being, but because they display the qualities that are most to be valued.

Both of the above approaches to the personal have value. It is a matter of common sense that part of what we respect in persons is a technical appreciation of the sheer range of possibilities associated with them. Their ability to communicate, to think, to show emotion and make judgements, whether or not they are of a different quality to the rest of creation, makes them more interesting. At the same time, there is also a sense that qualities like conscience and love are significant for more than technical reasons. It is as if by being able to make moral judgements people recognise, not simply an additional technical possibility, but something to which they wish to give ultimate significance.

For some philosophers of religion, it is this attitude towards morality, inbuilt as they see it into human beings, that makes theism necessary. God alone can guarantee that the moral desires of humanity are satisfied — for instance, by providing a life after death in which happiness can be proportioned to virtue, as it patently is not in this life. Such a view reminds us — as we shall see in greater detail in the next chapter — that there is an odd paradox where the 'moral' qualities of God are concerned. On the one hand there are those who are convinced that God cannot be good given the amount of injustice in the world. On the other hand are those convinced that the only explanation of such injustice must be the existence of God (for otherwise there would be no way of satisfying the human desire to see justice prevail).

Having looked at some of the reasons why God is thought of in personal terms, it is as well to remind ourselves of some of the dangers of doing so. One obvious problem is that such imagery may lead us to undervalue the significance of the impersonal, particularly if we treat it somehow as the valueless first rung on the ladder of being. Many people in the Western or Near Eastern traditions might indeed wonder whether there isn't a link between their neglect of the physical environment (something becoming increasingly obvious in the 'green' 1990s), and a tendency to relate to God simply as a 'person out there', unconnected to anything as 'denigrating' as matter.

In what ways, then, have philosophers of religion attempted to combine personal and impersonal imagery in order to represent the divine nature? One particular attempt needs to be examined carefully.

God's world, God's body?

One approach to the problem has been to think of the world as God's body. God is present throughout reality in the sense in which a person can be said to be present throughout his or her body. An attraction of this view is that the notion of the 'I' or 'self' appears to bear the character of transcendence and immanence, discussed at length in the previous section. The 'I' at one and the same time transcends the body (so that for instance we talk of our bodies as something separate from ourselves and say that we 'have' them rather than 'are' them) and is immanent or present in the body. Moreover, the 'I' or self is not present in a particular part of the body. This too, some have argued, makes it an apt image for God's presence in the world.

However, this analogy possesses two serious flaws. On the one hand, it is clear that we depend for survival upon our bodies, whereas we may not want to say that God depends upon the world for survival. In Christian tradition this has been very clearly stated. To revert to the early Christian analogy between the physical universe and a tune, the singer can survive without a song. More generally, creation has always been understood as an act of God's grace, something He could perfectly well have chosen not to do, rather than some kind of necessary mechanism through which He ensured His own existence. The relation between the world and God is not one of reciprocal dependence: the world exists only as an act of divine favour. God does not even 'need' the world in the sense imagined by those who suppose He must be lonely without it. Christians argue that the whole point about a tri-personal God is that the benefits of society, as well as those of individuality, are contained within the being of God. He does not need the world for company!

In the second place, the analogy fails to make any distinction between the way bodies behave and the way inanimate objects behave. It insists upon lumping the whole of reality together as a single 'thing' or 'system' like a body, rather than recognising that it is more a collection of different things, a network of interrelated but separate systems, animate and inanimate, that cannot be welded together into one 'thing'. The differences between objects and persons cannot be recognised properly if they are conceived of as different 'bits' of God's body.

Thus our argument against this way of conceiving God is twofold. First, it revokes the fundamental belief in a dependence of the world upon God that is not reciprocated by an equal and opposite dependence of God upon the world. Second, it actually overrides the differences between animate and inanimate, and thereby between the personal and impersonal, by perpetuating the myth of the universe as one big 'thing', usually thought of in personal terms — as in the idea of 'mother earth'. Once again, it may be the impersonal that is being undervalued by an approach that is effectively denying inanimate objects their autonomy by trying to present them virtually as the organs of God's body. The image of a body simply cannot do justice, we are saying, to the reality of — and our complex emotional reaction to — overpowering physical realities like the sea or the night-sky (however much we may be told that the stars are a twinkle in God's eye!).

What we have to do is to think of a personal God *without* thinking of a 'body' of God. This is one clear way in which we can recognise the clear distinction between the form of human personality and the form of divine personality. An image of God as a person like ourselves — for instance an old man on a cloud, or for that matter a young man from Nazareth — can, therefore, be deeply misleading. Personality is mediated at the human level through individual bodies. At the divine level, however, personality is expressed differently. Whereas human personality is present in bodies, divine personality is present in what is inanimate also. In conveying divine personality, therefore, impersonal images such as light are appropriate as well as personal images such as judge and father.

The impersonal imagery is essential if we are not to think of God as a person like ourselves. It prevents us falling back upon the familiar ideas of a 'father in heaven' who is thought of in much the same way as Santa Claus or an uncle in Australia. Without a means of preserving the difference between divine and human personality, we are liable to end up with an idea of God as a favourite uncle! Such an idea could easily be associated with domesticating and trivialising the Deity.

divine agency

Linked to the idea of a personal God is the notion of God as an historical agent. Some religious traditions emphasise that certain events in the world can be considered to be God's actions, and have claimed that what we know of God is derived from our interpretation of these events. What we know of other people is learned in a similar manner. Other people, for all that we may claim to understand them, still have an irreducibly transcendent 'core' — expressed in the fact that we can never enter their minds and think as they do. People reveal themselves in their actions, but they can never be reduced to them. In a similar way, the argument goes, God reveals Himself in particular events (that may themselves be the actions of His agents, like Jesus of Nazareth or Mohammed) but can never be reduced to them. We may see here a way of expressing the double motif of God's transcendence and immanence discussed above.

It may be — despite the fact that there are many incarnations or revelations of God in the Indian religious traditions too — that there is a difference here between some religious traditions of the Near East and those of the Indian sub-continent. Whilst both sets of traditions talk in personal terms of God, it seems that the Near Eastern religions, perhaps because of a stronger sense of historical progress, have developed further the idea of God as an historical agent — someone who has revealed His hand by associating with particular events and claiming them as His own. Whilst not retracting anything that has been said about the inappropriateness of either a corporeal God or a God who is a person, it has to be said that interpreting certain historical events as the actions of God is the primary way in which a number of religions understand the divine nature. For Judaism, God is the liberator who brought the Hebrew slaves out of Egypt and subsequently acted to protect and chastise them throughout their chequered history. For Christians, God's activity becomes associated not only with particular events but with a particular set of human actions, those that characterise what we know of the life of Jesus of Nazareth.

In the next chapter we will discuss the 'moral' qualities of God under the title: 'Is God Good?' It must be admitted that a great deal of what Judaeo-Christianity has to say about the 'goodness' of God is based upon claims about the way in which He involves himself in the historical process. Moreover, much of the moral imperative of Judaeo-Christianity, to love one's enemies, to support the poor and so on, is based upon the idea that God got His own divine hands dirty by becoming associated with actions that promoted such principles. Indeed Christianity might even say that in Jesus of Nazareth those actions were God's. The idea that God is good might owe a great deal in those traditions to a view that God has done good things in the world Himself — that God Himself is in some way an actor on the world stage.

But does the crucial significance of this understanding of divine agency require that we think of God as a person? Is it possible to make sense of revelation in any other way? Is it possible to associate God with particular events without such a presumption? Certainly such a relation of God with the world prevents us thinking of the physical universe in its entirety as God's 'body'. But are we left with a view of God as one of the actors on the world stage in the manner of the pagan gods, a benign Zeus who 'comes down' from Olympus to perform what is morally uplifting on earth? Can we understand divine agency without reducing God to a person like ourselves? This is the question that the Near Eastern religions in particular have to address, and that they often fail to answer. They have to find a way of expressing their confidence that God reveals Himself through His activity in the world, without making Him into a person like ourselves.

a definition of God

What sort of monster, if any, have we identified? Can we conclude that despite our reservations about Hick's presupposition that all religions believe in the same God, there is a case for seeing a common theistic structure among many of the world's religious traditions (or at least those that have any idea of God at all)?

In terms of a common form of theism, we have suggested that those world religions we have examined are all fundamentally monotheistic — they believe in one God. We have also suggested that they all conceive of God as both transcendent and immanent — transcendent in the sense that what fundamentally limits reality does not apply to Him, immanent in that this lack of limitation is what makes possible a universal presence. We have also suggested that this God is personal, but that the form of the divine personality is not that of human personality. God is not present in the way that we are present, in bodily form. God's presence extends throughout what is impersonal as well as what is personal.

We have tried to avoid in this chapter the sort of generalised waffle about God in which many theologians indulge. Take, for instance, this grotesque definition of God by Professor Keith Ward in his *Holding Fast to God*:

....God is infinitely potential: his is a dynamic power, from which an infinite set of new and different values can always arise. He is not just wholly complete and static, frozen into an eternal completeness. He is dynamic and creative, always moving on to new realisations of his infinite activity. God is the infinite potentiality for good. This is as far as you can get from Cupitt's picture of a reactionary, static super-tyrant [in his *Taking Leave of God*] always making sure the universe remains the same and conforms to the old unchanging laws.

Ward and Cupitt, two Christians angry with each other's definitions, swap epithets about static super-tyrants and dynamic powers, frozen gods and gods on the move, those that are reactionary and those that have infinite potentiality. But do we achieve any understanding of what their two different Gods are like from this conflict?

The difficulty with defining God is that the theist is perfectly entitled to claim that 'God' refers to something that cannot be known in the way that other things are known. At the same time, the atheist is perfectly entitled to claim that whether or not there is some special difficulty involved in defining 'God', anyone who uses the word must be clear about what he or she is saying. To say that God is incomprehensible invites the perfectly reasonable response from the philosopher of religion, Frederick Ferré (*Language, Logic and God*):

> One's only logically appropriate stand when confronted with incomprehensibility is a demand for clarification; belief, even with the best of good will, must wait upon the provision of a content to believe.

A very famous 'proof' of God's existence, the so-called 'Ontological Argument' associated with St Anselm, defines God as 'that than which nothing greater can be thought to exist'. Anselm's definition is seen as part of a clever philosophical con trick whereby he argues that it is greater for something to exist than not to exist, and thereby that the definition of God (as the greatest thing conceivable) demands that He exist! Few people find Anselm a serious contender for proving the existence of God, although there have been many philosophers who have rightly observed, as we have tried to do, that the logic of existence requires careful consideration. But what is less often pointed out is that Anselm in *The Proslogion* also defines God as 'greater than can be thought to exist'. In other words, where God is concerned we are attempting to think of that than which nothing greater can be thought, which is also *beyond* thought. In thinking of God, we are trying to think beyond the limits of thought. It is arguable that here Anselm is not thinking of God in terms very different from those of Kant, the severest critic of his 'Ontological Argument' (at least in the form in which it was mediated to him by Descartes).

Given that the theist believes that defining God involves thinking beyond the limits of thought, can he or she also fulfil the demand that a clear explanation be given of what is meant by the word 'God'? Cannot the sort of difficulty which the theist experiences in terms of describing God, for instance, as personal and impersonal, be justified by pointing out that attempting to think beyond the limits of thought is bound to entail stretching ordinary language beyond what it would normally bear? The theist thereby comes to justify as a paradox what the atheist is wont to dismiss as a confusion.

In this chapter I have deliberately not concentrated upon analysing lists of attributes. I have tried to make general observations about the structure of theism. Can these observations form the basis of a definition? For the atheist, they cannot. The problem may not be so much that when we talk of God we say nothing, as that we say too much — we say things that seem to combine irreconcilable images that can never be focussed upon one 'being'. Can the theist respond that he or she does have a coherent understanding of God? Can, for instance, the emphasis upon God as 'underlying reality', and upon God active in history as a personal agent, be regarded as compatible elements in an understanding of God common to many world religions?

In this chapter I have done more to highlight some of the problems in reaching a definition of God than to offer a solution of my own. The position I have tried to adopt is that whilst the atheist must demand clarity, the theist can argue that the nature of his or her task necessitates a use of language that is bound to be criticised as unusual, although it cannot be allowed to be contradictory. Whilst some theists like to bask in their own linguistic confusions, the more dangerous temptation is to pretend that some simple formula like 'love' or 'supreme being' — or even 'infinite potential' — can somehow solve all theological problems.

notes

Anselm, St (1033-1109) Born the son of a Lombard landowner, Anselm eventually became Archbishop of Canterbury in England. He had a very high reputation as a spiritual guide (he was for a time Abbot of Bec in Normandy) and teacher. His time at Canterbury led to constant tensions with the Crown and periods of exile in Rome. Apart from *The Proslogion* in which he propounded his 'Ontological Argument', Anselm wrote an important work entitled, *Why did God become Man? (Cur Deus Homo)*, regarded as a classic in Christian writings about the 'atonement' (the means by which, after the Fall, God is once more reconciled to humanity).

Aquinas, St Thomas (1225-1274) A medieval theologian whose thought (Thomism) has been more profoundly influential upon Christian (particularly Roman Catholic) thinking than any other. Aquinas sought systematically to bring the worlds of philosophy and theology together. In particular he thought that the fundamental principles of Aristotle's philosophy could provide a setting in which to express the revealed truths of Christian faith.

Kant, Immanuel (1724-1804) Although one of the most difficult of all philosophers to read, Kant is one of the most important for theologians to examine. His most significant work, *The Critique of Pure Reason*, sets out the limits to thought insofar as they can ever be set from the perspective of people who are subject to those limits themselves. His *Religion Within the Limits of Reason Alone* expounds what he saw as the ethical basis of religion. His life was one of unambitious regularity. He lived and died in Königsberg, never venturing beyond the province, and had the reputation of being the contented bachelor from whose afternoon walk it was possible to set one's watch. Though his thought may have been in some respects dry and narrow as a result, he set the agenda for modern philosophy and theology. Some would see his agnosticism, his awareness of the limits to thought, as the only true basis for religious faith.

Paley, William (1743-1805) Though highly skilled as a lecturer in mathematics and ethics, Paley is best-known for his *Evidences of Christianity*, published in 1794, and for his *Natural Theology* published in 1802. His confidence that God's existence could be demonstrated from the natural world made him a favourite target for those who felt it could only be on the basis of God's special revelation of Himself that faith could be justified.

further reading

Professor Sallie McFague's *Models of God* examines a number of ideas of the divine nature, including God as mother, lover and friend. She explores the idea of the world as God's body, an idea which received earlier treatment by Grace Jantzen in her *God's World, God's Body*.

Neither Jantzen nor McFague really gets to grips with the philosophical issues involved. A theologian who does (though from a more conservative perspective) is E.L. Mascall. In his *He Who Is: A Study in Traditional Theism* (intended as a response to Martin Buber's *I and Thou*) and in his work *Existence and Analogy*, Mascall sets out the main arguments of the Thomist. His careful exploration of existence, the self and God in these books is uncritical of Aquinas, but shows a sophisticated awareness of the problems involved in defining God, and an awareness of the dangers involved in 'using models'.

In this book I have tried to move beyond the Judaeo-Christian tradition in the discussion. My claim has been that there are parallels to be observed between the theism of the Western religious traditions and that of the main Eastern religious tradition. The further reading in this area is enormous. The spectrum of religious beliefs is best approached initially through compendia: for instance the *Concise Encyclopaedia of Living Faiths*, edited by R.C. Zaehner, or the more recent *Handbook of Living Religions*, edited by John R. Hinnells (which has bibliographies for each religious tradition). It is vitally important to know something of the individual richness and variety of each religious tradition before becoming subject to the generalisations of those engaged in comparative religion.

5: is God good?

the evil genius

It is possible to divide the qualities or attributes of God into two kinds: 'natural' and 'moral'. The natural qualities are characteristics such as eternity, omniscience, omnipotence and infinity; the moral qualities are characteristics such as wisdom, justice, mercy and love. In this chapter we shall concentrate upon the second set of qualities, asking the question: Is God good?

There is sometimes a tendency to take it for granted that any god who existed would be good. It is assumed that the existence of God must be of benefit to humankind. But *can* we take this for granted? The idea of an 'evil genius' explores the possibility that God's existence is very bad news for us all!

It is useful to introduce a further distinction which is often made in this sort of discussion. This concerns the difference between what is termed 'natural evil' and 'moral evil'. The former concerns the pain and suffering that is seen as occurring naturally, such as disease or loss of life from an earthquake. 'Moral evil', on the other hand, concerns the suffering inflicted by one person on another by a deliberate act of will, for instance in war.

It is important to point out that this distinction is not as clear-cut as it is sometimes made out to be. Take the case of earthquakes. Human beings are not responsible for them directly, but a lot of countries that suffer huge loss of life from them do so because they do not bother to erect buildings that are relatively secure from their effects. Or take disease. Is there no 'moral evil' involved in human responsibility for increasing the likelihood of cancer, for instance, by nuclear testing or by promoting tobacco? This is not to say for one moment that responsibility for the suffering caused by disease and natural disasters can be laid entirely at the door of human beings. At the same time, however, it is all too easy to forget the human share of responsibility when labelling such tragedies in the words of the insurance companies as 'acts of God'.

The distinction between 'natural evil' and 'moral evil', even though the boundary between them is not easy to draw, allows us to consider whether the goodness of God is more compromised by one than the other. It might be said, for instance, that 'moral evil' can at least be laid fairly and squarely at the door of human beings. They cause suffering; they must be held responsible for it. But even here there exists the further question of how presumably an all-powerful God can allow human beings to inflict such suffering upon one another. For instance, if you come across someone being beaten up in a street and do not try to intervene, it could be said that you are partly responsible for the suffering of the victim. Yet God, who has the added advantage of being able to intervene without being beaten up Himself, apparently chooses not to do so. Can He escape responsibility?

The enormous amount of suffering that has characterised the history of the human race prompts the imagination to consider an alternative scenario to that offered by the optimism of most theists. Suppose that we were created not by a 'good' God but by a 'bad' God. Perhaps this God was a bored sadist, whose mastery of the universe was tiresome without the relief of being able to inflict pain and confusion upon this and perhaps other worlds as a form of amusement. The evil genius created the earth much as a Roman emperor might have designed an amphitheatre. Onto the earth, which He looks down upon much as the rulers of Imperial Rome looked down upon the arena, he placed a large number of creatures whose lives were dominated by constant and bloody battle against each other. These were the gladiators. As a particular refinement, however, this God created one species that had the capacity not only to kill but to kill with sophistication, to torture to death. This species always provided the highlight at any gladiatorial show.

Such a view would deny that there is an overall moral development in history. The species referred to as the climax of creation, humanity, would be recognised as having achieved a great deal by way of technical refinement over the centuries. The argument would be that it has made great strides intellectually, but has never progressed morally. This is not surprising, since the evil genius had no interest in moral development, only in enjoying greater and greater refinements of cruelty. This God had the sort of mentality of those humans who go out of their way to buy 'snuff' movies which feature people being killed, or gather round fights in the street because their lives are given extra spice by the sight of violent brutality. Thus the most recent century on earth reveals, in accordance with the wishes of the evil genius, an even greater level of cruelty than previous ones, culminating in the systematic attempt to exterminate a race which succeeded in killing approximately six million people.

Some would say that this is a distorted picture of human development. Others might see it as a useful challenge to the sort of cosy assurance that we *are* making progress, which often confuses technical with moral development. At the very least it makes clear that even if we accept direct human responsibility for much of the suffering in our world, we still have to consider what sort of a God permits such suffering, even if we accept that He is not directly responsible for it.

Then there is the question of 'natural evil'. This provides what to many people is an even greater challenge to the goodness of God. In a well-known collection of articles entitled *New Essays in Philosophical Theology*, the philosopher Antony Flew writes as follows:

> Someone tells us that God loves us as a father loves his children. We are reassured. But then we see a child dying of inoperable cancer of the throat. His earthly father is driven frantic in his efforts to help, but his Heavenly Father reveals no obvious sign of concern. Some qualification is made — God's love is 'not a merely human love' or it is 'an inscrutable love'.... We are reassured again. But then perhaps we ask: what is this assurance of God's (apparently qualified) love worth?

Whether it is the suffering we deliberately inflict upon each other, or the suffering which appears to be imposed on us by nature (such as disease), there are many who would agree with Antony Flew that it is irreconcilable with belief in God's goodness. God is supposed to take a delight in Creation. According to Judaeo-Christian tradition, God looked down on the world that had been made and saw that it was 'very good' (Genesis

1:31). Some would say that to look down on a world with a history of suffering such as ours has had and find it 'very good' is compatible only with a mentality that enjoys the pain of others. The God who looks down on us, they would say, is the evil genius whose technical mastery is invested in creating something to amuse his sadistic interests. It is not the loving Father of Christian tradition.

In the Sermon on the Mount, Jesus of Nazareth is credited with the words:

> What man of you, if his son asks him for bread, will give him a stone? Or if he asks for a fish, will give him a serpent? If you then, who are evil, know how to give good gifts to your children, how much more will your Father who is in heaven give good things to those who ask him.

> (Matthew 7:9-11)

Antony Flew's example of childhood cancer puts a question mark against this interpretation. Many earthly fathers behave a lot more cruelly towards their children than those who feed their offspring in this passage from the Christian gospel. But few of them behave with such apparent cruelty or neglect as the heavenly Father who allows thousands of children to die agonising deaths from cancer and other diseases throughout the world.

For many people it is the impossibility of believing that God is good, rather than of believing that God exists, which alienates them from religion. They follow the example of Ivan Karamazov in Dostoevsky's famous novel *The Brothers Karamazov*. Ivan Karamazov cited a long list of instances of human cruelty and suffering to his brother Alyosha. He included the example of a huntsman who delighted in setting his hounds upon children rather than foxes. He asks Alyosha how a good God can permit such things to happen. Alyosha replies (in the manner of the example cited by Flew above, where he talks of those who say that God's love is 'different' from ours) that he cannot claim to fathom the ways of God. So Ivan asks him: Would you, if you were God, permit such things to happen? Alyosha has to admit that he would not. Ivan concludes that he admires his humane brother Alyosha, and admits that he might consent to live in a world made by him. But in no way will Ivan live in the world made by God. In Dostoevsky's famous image, Ivan offers to return this God his ticket. God can give it to someone more willing than Ivan to appreciate the show on display.

The debate about God's goodness is another aspect of the debate introduced earlier in the book, namely: What is God? In the next two chapters I will try to examine ways in which religion has attempted to give a moral character to God that has made the divine being worthy of worship rather than contempt. What reason is there, even if God exists, to be a worshipper rather than, like Lucifer in Christian tradition, someone who rebels? Is God obeyed and adored only because He is too strong to be resisted? If so, should we not take every step to oppose such a deity, even in the condition of weakness which we find ourselves in? Even if the result of such opposition should be eternal torment at the hands of the evil genius, would we not resist anyway? Even if the prospect is hell in the afterlife, should we not do something to frustrate the efforts of the evil genius to create a hell on earth?

retribution or reform? the case of original sin

In the next two sections we shall examine several attempted solutions to what has been classically termed 'the problem of evil'. In the case of the first religion which we consider, Christianity, the problem is particularly severe because in this case the reality of evil has to be rendered compatible with the existence of a good God. In the second religion we examine, Buddhism, this difficulty does not arise, since we are dealing here with a non-theistic religion that is indifferent to the question of God's existence.

Christianity does not have a single approach to the problem. The two Christian traditions under examination will be supplemented in a further section by study of an approach denying that any solution to the problem of evil can be offered. This approach can also claim to exist within the Christian religion. It has to be recognised that an individual religion may contain a variety of different and even competing traditions, which makes it necessary for us at times to treat of the same religion in the context of advancing very different and even incompatible arguments about God.

Both Christian traditions examined here attempt to demonstrate why the goodness of God may be reconciled with the existence of evil. One tradition treats evil as a punishment for sin, and the other treats it as a means by which human beings are educated. These two have sometimes been labelled 'Augustinian' and 'Irenaean', after the two early church writers, Augustine and Irenaeus, with whom they are associated. It should be borne in mind, however, that both traditions can be found in the writings of each of these theologians, although broadly speaking the first tradition is found more in Augustine and the second more in Irenaeus.

The first tradition argues that evil in the world is a consequence of its 'fallen' condition, and that it is therefore the responsibility of human beings because it was they who gave in to temptation and fell. Suffering is therefore a divine punishment, and did not exist in Paradise before Adam and Eve ate from the tree of the knowledge of good and evil in the Garden of Eden.

> In Paradise, then, man...lived without any want, and had it in his power so to live eternally. He had food that he might not hunger, drink that he might not thirst, the tree of life that old age might not waste him. There was in his body no corruption, nor seed of corruption, which could produce in him any unpleasant sensation. He feared no inward disease, no outward accident. Soundest health blessed his body, absolute tranquillity his soul. As in Paradise there was no excessive heat or cold, so its inhabitants were exempt from the vicissitudes of fear and desire. No sadness of any kind was there, nor any foolish joy; true gladness ceaselessly flowed from the presence of God....

This tradition does not question that the combination of physical comfort and mental harmony described by Augustine in the *City of God* is desirable. It has none of the doubts of those who feel that pleasure cannot exist without its opposite, pain, or that without experience of sadness there could be no joy. It describes the sort of world that many people would regard as precisely what God would have created were He really good — a world in which there was none of the strife and pain that characterise life on earth. But having painted a glowing picture of the very different, desirable and pain-free world in which we could be living, Augustine then attempts to defend the goodness of a God who has created the very different world in which we actually find ourselves living. His defence is that we deserve such a world as punishment for sin.

We shall not enter here into the complex arguments concerning the nature of original sin, the way in which we may be held co-responsible with Adam and Eve for that sin, or the extent to which God 'foreknew' their decision to eat from the tree. We shall simply concentrate upon the idea that this world contains suffering that it could well do without because of an act of divine retribution. Does this enable us to avoid the divine sadist idea? Does it make it easier for us to say that God is good? It is difficult to see how it does. Even if human beings did do something outrageous in the Garden of Eden, does an omnipotent God bear no responsibility for allowing them to do it? And even if it is a matter of freedom that human beings should be allowed to act outrageously if they choose to do so, is God justified in punishing them with what appears to be an indefinitely lasting environment of suffering? The problem for those who seek to exonerate God through the argument that suffering is a punishment for original sin is this. Given the severity of the punishment which He metes out for an obscure act of resistance to His will in the Garden of Eden, does God appear any better on the basis of this scenario than a God who simply inflicts suffering on the basis of a sadistic whim? We find ourselves not so much with a sadist as with a tyrant who cannot bear to be crossed by anyone and never forgives those who once did so (nor their descendants). But this only means that we end up with one form of unpleasantness in the Deity rather than another.

The second tradition within Christianity argues that the expulsion of Adam and Eve from the Garden of Eden was not so much a punishment as the sort of process by which parents might suggest to their adolescent offspring that it was time they left home and attempted to live on their own. Such a move is not so much a punishment as a way of encouraging greater maturity. The distance between God and humanity, which according to the first tradition is a distance set by God in banishing men and women from the divine presence, is here more a process of granting them 'space' in which to survive on their own and become more independent. In an allusion made by Irenaeus, humanity in the Garden of Eden is like the babe fed on milk; but after a while it has to learn to eat meat (Irenaeus did not seem to have heard of vegetarianism!):

For as it certainly is in the power of a mother to give strong food to her infant [but she does not do so] as the child is not yet able to receive more substantial nourishment; so also it was possible for God Himself to have made man perfect from the first, but man could not receive this [perfection], being as yet an infant.

The Irenaean tradition within Christianity might seem to be a better one. God becomes the reformer or educator of humanity rather than its punisher. And Irenaeus is aware of a problem with the sort of description Augustine offered above of a pain-free Paradise:

How, if we had no knowledge of the contrary, could he [humanity] have had instruction in that which is good? For just as the tongue receives experience of sweet and bitter by means of tasting, and the eye discriminates between black and white by means of vision, and the ear recognises the distinction of sounds by hearing; so also does the mind, receiving through the experience of both the knowledge of what is good, become more tenacious of its preservation, by acting in obedience to God....But if anyone do shun the knowledge of both kinds of things, and the twofold perception of knowledge, he unawares divests himself of the character of a human being.

Irenaeus suggests in these references from his *Against Heresies* that had we never left Augustine's Paradise we would never have been fully human. We would not have been able to learn to make the sort of moral judgements that allow us to mature as men and women. Irenaeus' view of the myth of the Garden of Eden, then, is determined to understand it in an educative rather than a punitive light. We might point out that his interpretation, which has a smaller following within Christianity than Augustine's, is the dominant one within Judaism. English versions of the Hebrew Bible (Old Testament) describe the serpent which entices Adam and Eve to eat from the tree as 'cunning'. But the Hebrew word is rather more positive than these translations suggest. The serpent is intelligent. One word employed by English versions is 'wily', a term used in a positive light by the New Testament when Jesus gives instructions to his disciples to be 'wily as serpents and innocent as doves'. Christian descriptions of the serpent as the purely evil force of Satan in disguise are not those of Judaism, the religious tradition within which the Genesis text was written.

But to return to the philosophical issue. How successful is Irenaeus' approach likely to be? Certainly the point that without experience of pain there could be no experience of pleasure has often been made. It has also been argued that individuals grow through the experience of suffering. But can these observations, which do suggest a certain naivety in the Augustinian picture of Paradise, offer a full defence of the idea that a good God could tolerate the amount of pain and evil that exists on earth?

Some suffering does educate. People are said to 'learn from their mistakes'. Pain can sometimes give a greater appreciation of life. The mental pain brought about by a bad conscience could be viewed in a positive light as a means of realising greater personal maturity. Natural disasters could be said to bring out a community spirit and acts of generosity as people attempt to respond to them. But how much of the pain and suffering in the world can be interpreted in this way? And how far is it in danger of a sentimentality that grossly underestimates the sheerly destructive effects of suffering?

There is a danger of such sentimentality where both 'natural evil' and 'moral evil' are concerned. Take 'natural evil'. Would those who care for the mentally ill or the chronically sick or the dying be as sure of the educative value of suffering as those, for instance, who have come through a sudden acute illness with the realisation that life was brief and should be appreciated whilst it lasts? What of those who have to cope with seeing relatives grow senile and lose their dignity? Or people who have to cope with the suffering of those whose pain is all the worse because they can hardly communicate about it, such as animals or young children?

The same question mark hangs over the value of 'moral evil'. Has, for instance, the world learned to be more tolerant because of the extermination of millions in the death camps? Does not that extermination in the most recent century of our history show that none of the suffering inflicted by human beings on each other in previous centuries had any real educative value? Has it made us any better since? What of the millions who have since been exterminated through the agency of Pol Pot? Generalisations must be avoided, but the evidence of progress is hard to establish. And even if an educative value *can* be identified, has the price of whatever tolerance and understanding we might have learned not been too high? To return to the point made by Ivan to Alyosha, which of us in our enthusiasm that people should understand themselves and the world around them better would consent to the suffering, murder, torture and death that would appear to be the condition of such understanding? Alyosha in Dostoevsky's novel has to admit that the death of a single child was not a price worth paying. He has to admit that even if some sort of good ultimate purpose can be identified for the suffering in the world, there remains the key question of whether the end justifies the means.

The Irenaean tradition, then, may not altogether remove the charge of 'evil genius' from God. Instead of the pure sadist or the tyrant who cannot bear to be crossed, we now have a ruler whose designs for human self-improvement are to be realised at any cost. Where Augustine gives us a Hitler, Irenaeus gives us a Stalin, whose vision of a better humanity is to be realised whatever the price. Especially from the perspective of the 1990s, it hardly seems to be much of an improvement.

is suffering real or unjust? the Buddhist case

The Buddhist religion offers a very different perspective upon suffering. Despite the fact that its various traditions are either indifferent or hostile towards the existence of God, they are deeply aware of the existence of suffering. It was the experience of human suffering that led the founder of Buddhism away from home, family, wealth and royal position to seek to share enlightenment with others. And it was his firm belief that he could identify both the causes of suffering and the means of overcoming it. Take this quotation from the first sermon of the Buddha at Benares:

> The Noble Truth of suffering is this: Birth is suffering; ageing is suffering; sickness is suffering; death is suffering; sorrow and lamentation, pain, grief and despair are suffering; association with the unpleasant is suffering; dissociation from the pleasant is suffering; not to get what one wants is suffering — in brief, the five aggregates of attachment are suffering.
>
> The Noble Truth of the origin of suffering is this: It is this thirst [craving] which produces re-existence and re-becoming, bound up with passionate greed. It finds fresh delight now here and now

there, namely, thirst for sense-pleasures; thirst for existence and becoming; and thirst for non-existence [self-annihilation].

The Noble Truth of the Cessation of suffering is this; complete cessation of that very thirst, giving it up, renouncing it, emancipating oneself from it, detaching oneself from it.

The suffering referred to includes both personal pain and a sense of ultimate meaninglessness in the universe. The solution of self-detachment in the quotation above has to be treated carefully, because Buddhism denies that there is an unchanging 'I' or 'self' which remains the eternal manager of experience. There is, however, in human awareness the possibility of achieving some limited control over a part of life, and this is to be encouraged.

The Buddhist rejection of the idea of a continuous self is important where it comes to considering the fact that, unlike the Near Eastern religions, Buddhism appears to believe in reincarnation or rebirth. It certainly does believe in life after death; but it does not say that this will be life for an unchanging 'I' who becomes attached to a new body and set of experiences in much the same way that a messenger might once have stopped at a staging-post in order to exchange his exhausted horse for a fresh one.

Despite this reluctance to speak of a continuous self, the Buddhist doctrine of Karma insists upon a chain of causation according to which every instance of suffering is the result of some cause earlier in the life-chain. Thus the Buddha explained the violent death of the righteous Moggallana by saying that he died in this way as a consequence of having beaten his parents at a previous moment in the chain of existence. It might not be right to say the chain of 'his' existence, which would imply too strong a notion of the continuing self. The most that would be claimed is that the two events, the death of the parents and the fate of Moggallana, were related as cause and effect. On the other hand, it might seem as if this connection could only make sense on the basis of presuming the continuing identity of the individual through a series of lives. This raises problems which would take us too far away from the main point, but it is fair to say that they must be faced by any philosophical explanation of the Buddhist position.

An answer to the question of why some people are rich and others poor, some beautiful and some ugly, some die young and others experience a ripe old age, is offered by drawing an analogy to the natural world. The variations between trees, for instance, can be traced back to differences in the seeds from which they grow. Similarly, there are 'seeds' in the past for the variations in wealth, looks, talent and so on between human beings which might otherwise appear quite arbitrary. Although this analogy might seem to imply that no-one has any freedom to determine his or her own life, the Buddhist religion insists that acts of will are seen as part of the 'chain of existence'. The process by which history develops, even if comparable to the manner in which little acorns give rise to tall mighty oaks, is one which includes the acts of will by which human beings realise one outcome rather than another.

Again there are important philosophical issues here which cannot be developed now. If we have free will, does that not make analogies between human history and biological processes, such as the way in which trees grow, misleading? Can acts of will simply be 'inserted' into the analogy to the growth of trees? These are not questions that can be discussed further here, but are obvious points which must be raised in any full discussion of the philosophical basis of Buddhism.

The Buddhist tradition, then, claims to offer an explanation of what has often been regarded as the aspect of suffering that makes it incompatible with belief in the goodness of God, namely its injustice. Buddhism offers a way of saying that no one suffers unjustly. So long as a wide enough perspective is taken, one that moves beyond this particular round on the wheel of life, apparently unjust events in the present can be shown to have reasonable cause in the past.

But there is a second way in which Buddhism approaches the problem of evil. For even 'just' suffering could be viewed as lacking in mercy. Even if Moggallana dies a violent death only because of the way his parents died, this might not necessarily be viewed as exonerating God from accusations of evil. Even if suffering is not arbitrary, even if there is a pattern which allows it to be said that it is 'deserved', still the pain involved might be regarded as excessive, and the whole process of suffering being visited upon oneself in consequence of visiting it on others could be seen as barbaric. Here the second aspect of the Buddhist approach becomes significant. For not only does it appear to deny the injustice of suffering, it also appears to offer a way through suffering that ultimately denies its reality.

Buddhism believes in the possibility of realising nirvana — the cessation of suffering — here and now. Nirvana is a freedom from the longing and craving which make human beings, in whatever situation they find themselves, suffer pain. It is a state not of annihilation but of reality, in which the passions and desires that cause suffering do not exist, a state of detachment from all those things that make suffering possible. When the Buddha abandoned his advantages in life, it was in order to teach this possibility of 'enlightenment', which provides a final release from 'samsara', the endless wheel of life. The state of enlightenment is one in which the individual has removed all the causes of suffering from himself or herself. The self is not anaesthetised, but rather enters a higher reality than that in which it suffers pain.

Once more, we can only mention in passing that there are philosophical questions raised by this claim. But one point in defence of Buddhism must be made clear. It is sometimes supposed, from the emphasis upon self-realisation which appears to be implicit in the talk of achieving enlightenment, that Buddhism is a religion with a merely selfish message. This would be untrue. As already stated the Buddha himself sacrificed advantages of wealth and status to share enlightenment with others. It is true that Buddhism teaches a way to personal fulfilment, but so do all religions. Is Christianity selfish because Jesus offers individuals rewards in heaven or indeed tells them how to have eternal life on earth? The compassion of the Buddha is as evident from what historical details are available as is the compassion of Jesus. Nor can it be said that this compassion merely expresses itself in a series of mental exercises unrelated to the giving of practical assistance. Buddhist tradition also emphasises specific action to relieve suffering. It is not a religion that can simply be dismissed as an exercise in spiritual self-indulgence.

The perspective upon suffering offered by Buddhism as a non-theistic religion provides an interesting contrast to that offered by the Near Eastern religions. It makes two important claims. First, that despite the apparent injustice of suffering there is always an answer to the question so often asked by the sufferer: Why me? Second, that whatever the suffering, and whatever the need to treat it by using any practical means available, there is a more fundamental way of overcoming the suffering. It is always possible to withdraw to a point where the suffering no longer touches the self, hard though the process of learning that process of withdrawal may be. It is not a withdrawal from reality, but a withdrawal from suffering *to* reality. And in that sense it seems fair to say that Buddhism not only denies the injustice of suffering but also its capacity to destroy the individual.

The contrast between Buddhism and Christianity demonstrated in these last two sections raises a number of issues. The two religions have very different approaches to answering the problem of evil. Buddhism might be thought to have the most radical and sophisticated answers, yet interestingly offers them in the context of a tradition which doesn't believe in God at all. The traditions that we have so far looked at from within Christianity set out to reconcile suffering with a form of theism. In their case the wider perspective on offer is not that of previous or future lives but that of the divine purpose. And in their very commitment to the punitive or educative intention of the Deity, they are not led to deny or lessen in any way the impact of suffering upon the individual — a charge that some might level at the Buddhist idea of enlightenment.

In the next section, we shall examine another approach to the problem of evil, one that represents an important tradition within the Near Eastern religions. So far we have looked at several attempted solutions. The tradition now under examination proclaims that there is no solution, but attempts nonetheless to maintain a traditional theistic perspective.

God's answer to Job: should he have accepted it?

In the Near Eastern religions there is little to parallel the answers offered to the problem of evil by Buddhism.

I should mention a minor tradition within Christianity associated with the early church writer Origen. Origen put forward a doctrine of pre-existence and reincarnation. Unlike Buddhism, his doctrine clearly presented the idea of a continuous soul travelling through a series of lives and receiving in each a due reward for its behaviour in previous lives. Origen was a universalist, believing that everyone would be saved in the end, even the Devil (who was, after all, only a fallen angel). The series of lives through which everyone passed on their way to heaven might be compared to a series of classes in a school. Everyone graduates in the end, but some have to spend longer in the lower forms than others. Apparent injustice in this life simply reflected that relative backwardness.

Within their mainstream traditions, however, none of the Near Eastern religions has been attracted by this explanation of the injustice of suffering. They have ruled out ideas of pre-existence and reincarnation. There may be a future judgement by God upon humanity after death, but one based upon behaviour in this life alone. These religions assert this despite the obvious problems which it brings, for instance in terms of imagining any sort of 'judgement' upon those millions of the world's inhabitants who died before the age of five. The Near Eastern religions insist upon presenting the brief moment astride of the grave which we live in this world as the only basis for determining our ultimate destinies. Perhaps traditions within these religions that attempt to soften this presentation — for instance Roman Catholic ideas of purgatory — reflect the difficulty many have with it.

Where Buddhism can explain the violent death of Moggallana in terms of his having beaten his parents at a previous time in the chain of existence, a religion like Christianity has no prospect of offering such an explanation, assuming that it rejects the approach of Origen outlined above. It may, of course, adopt the sort of generalised explanations of suffering in terms of divine retribution or divine education outlined two sections above. But these fall down as soon as the discussion moves from the general to the particular, and we are confronted by instances of unproductive and meaningless suffering. This leaves a God who over-punishes or crushes everything beneath the juggernaut of a dubious educational purpose. Outside the cosy confines of the faithful, few people are likely to be convinced by such an approach.

There remains one further approach. This is to deny that there is any explanation for suffering at all, either for the intensity and inescapability of the experience of it or for the injustice of its distribution. It is arguable that an important tradition within the Near Eastern religions offers no explanation of injustice whatsoever — indeed it specifically condemns attempts to find an explanation. Incidentally, it is true that Christianity has a powerful tradition ascribing evil to an adversary of God, Satan or Lucifer, but this tradition is quite aberrant despite its following. Judaism and Islam, which recognise clearly how the sovereignty of God cannot admit room for some kind of divine opponent, have never been tempted in this direction to the same extent. But even Christianity has to admit that ascribing evil to Satan falls into the trap of denying God's omnipotence. If Christians then try to assert that God 'allows' Satan to bring evil upon the world, then they can no longer maintain God's goodness. They merely substitute for a sadist who acts directly a sadist who allows his henchman to do his dirty work for him.

The Book of Job in the Hebrew Bible (Old Testament) provides a key text for Jewish and Christian interpretations of injustice. Job suffers the loss of his possessions, health and family. It leads him to curse the day of his birth and to find no meaning or justice in life. He then encounters a number of advisers who have given the expression 'Job's Comforters' to our culture — in other words people whose 'comfort' is false and unhelpful. Each of these advisers denies that there is any injustice in life and insists that Job's suffering and that of his family must be a consequence of their sins (and those of their ancestors, for they claim that God visits the sins of the fathers upon the children). Eliphaz the Temanite asks rhetorically, 'Who that was innocent ever perished?' (Job 4:4); Bildad the Shuhite suggests that the death of Job's children is a consequence of their sins (Job 8:4); Zophar the Naamathite echoes the others in suggesting that suffering is evidence of sin, and in no way suggests any sort of injustice in the ways of God towards men and women.

Job persists in asking for an explanation of suffering and rejects the ideas of his 'comforters' that suffering is always precisely proportioned to sin and therefore expresses a recognisable divine justice. Job cannot see this, and insists upon calling for God to appear like a witness in a court to answer his questions.

At the end of the book Job receives an answer of sorts. God speaks to him, but only in order to remind him of the distance between creature and Creator:

Where were you when I laid the foundations of the earth?
Tell me, if you have understanding.
Who determined its measurements — surely you know!
Or who stretched the line upon it?
On what were its bases sunk,
or who laid its cornerstone,
when the morning stars sang together,
and all the sons of God shouted for joy?

(Job 38:4-7)

The argument appears to be that the ways of God are so far beyond human understanding that they cannot be justified to men and women. It is with this conclusion that the Book of Job ends. It is important to point out that Job's 'comforters', who believed that they could explain suffering as proportionate to wickedness, are rebuked by God: 'My wrath is kindled against you...'(Job 42:7). Job, on the other hand, accepts God's answer and is rewarded with wealth, new sons and daughters and long life: 'Job died, an old man, and full of days' (Job 42:17). The Book of Job apparently seeks to tell us that the world is a mystery and the ways of God so far beyond human understanding that they cannot be made clear to us, either by human beings like Eliphaz, Bildad and Zophar or by direct revelation from God.

This denial of an explanation by the Near Eastern religions is interesting. The reality of undeserved suffering in the world has led many people to follow Ivan Karamazov in rejecting God even if one should exist. Religious traditions like Buddhism have attempted to suggest that from a wider perspective apparently undeserved suffering *is* in fact deserved, and this has at times been attempted as an argument within Judaism and Christianity (the Book of Job was undoubtedly written in order to reject such arguments that must have been in evidence at the time — and in the Christian era there was a powerful following for the Origenist position). But is the refusal of an answer likely to produce in us the reaction of pious humility that it seemed to engender in Job? That must be open to question.

Certainly there is one powerful argument that has been offered by supporters of the 'There is no explanation' school. They have suggested that where the 'natural' qualities of God are concerned, such as eternity, infinity and omniscience, we seem to be prepared to conceive that our understanding of the divine being, if it exists, must be limited. God, if there is one, must be beyond human comprehension. A God so brought down to our size as to be clearly imaginable, this argument goes, would not be God. Some cash value must be given to the idea of God's transcendence.

But if this is true of the 'natural' qualities of God, they say, why not also of the 'moral' qualities? Why should not the wisdom, mercy, justice, love and goodness of God be as hard to fathom as the eternity and omniscience of the Deity? Why in the moral sphere, do we insist upon the sort of clear understanding that we may be prepared to deny ourselves in the natural sphere? Is not the process of giving up the idea that God can be good in the way that human beings are good rather like the process of giving up the idea that God is like an old man on a cloud? It is the same process, this argument would run, of learning not to impose upon the divine being images, be they natural or moral, drawn from our own human experience.

However, we have already highlighted some of the difficulties involved in the simple assertion that God is too far beyond our comprehension for us to say anything about Him. The main problem is that those who take this line, in fact, *do* say a great deal about God. They pin a number of labels on Him such as 'eternal', 'omniscient', 'infinite', and then when we ask for definitions of these terms they fall back upon the argument that God is beyond understanding. It would seem that they must either assert the incomprehensibility of God and say nothing about His nature at all, or justify their description of God by admitting that His nature, to some degree at least, *can* be understood.

Precisely the same form of argument can be applied in the area of God's moral qualities. We can say with Job that it is impossible to fathom the ways of God towards humanity. In which case it must be impossible to call Him 'just' rather than 'unjust', 'wise' rather than 'foolish', 'loving' rather than 'filled with hate'. We are left admitting that we are quite in the dark so far as the moral nature of God is concerned. On the other hand, if we wish to join with the Judaeo-Christian tradition in asserting that God is indeed wise, loving, just, merciful and good, then we must surely offer some evidence as to why we do so. We cannot have our cake and eat it. Either we don't know whether God is good, or we do know and can say why we know.

Moreover, the suggestion that we can affirm the justice of God, without any requirement to say how we understand the nature of the divine justice, enables us in effect to give God carte blanche to be as unpleasant from a human perspective as He likes, and offers to His earthly interpreters the opportunity to make Him as unpleasant as they like! We find an illustration of this in the Christian tradition, if we consider John Calvin's famous doctrine of predestination, according to which God predetermined certain individuals to eternal life and others to eternal perdition before they were born (indeed, to be precise, before God even made the world). Calvin agreed that by any human criterion such a doctrine was immoral, but he believed it to be warranted by Scripture and by what he saw as the implicit requirements of a doctrine of divine omnipotence (according to which God must determine exactly who is to be saved before they are born, since an omnipotent God can hardly 'wait and see how they turn out'). If it were immoral — in fact if it were an example of abhorrent unfairness to most human beings — that was because God's justice was different from ours. That was all that could and indeed all that needed to be said in the face of the criticism that the doctrine of predestination made God out to be an arbitrary tyrant.

The fact that the 'Job solution' appears to have released many theists from any inhibitions they might otherwise have felt towards painting God in the most tyrannical light is itself at least a cautionary argument against it. What we discover is that when God's justice is said to be beyond our understanding, then even what appears from a human perspective to be gross *in*justice can be said to be from a divine perspective justice. The door is opened to the sort of theology we find in Calvin, one which is prepared to ignore all human criteria of goodness and justice in its efforts to follow what it sees to be the logic of its own doctrinal position. It is scant surprise that a number of people brought up in such a tradition turn against what they see as the immorality of Christianity long before they find any other objections to it. But at the risk of arrogance in dismissing what has plainly been a deeply attractive religious position to millions and remains so, the Calvinist tradition is absurd. If what to humans is unjust is said to be in God's eyes just, then we plainly say nothing meaningful about God at all when we call Him just, and have no entitlement to do so.

The position of Job appears to leave us in a position where we cannot apply any moral epithet to God whatsoever. God is neither good nor bad, just nor unjust, wise nor foolish. God is God. We could, of course, follow Calvin and *define* justice as 'what God wills', but this sleight of hand doesn't really help us with the moral qualities of God either. We remove the concept of 'justice' from the meaning it is given within human experience, and effectively end up with a statement whose content is no greater than 'God wills what God wills'. We effectively renounce any claim to be able to make sense of God's goodness, mercy, justice, wisdom or love, on the basis of what counts as good, merciful, just, wise or loving actions on the part of men and women in their ordinary lives. We say, in effect: 'Viewed from the perspective of what we understand these qualities to be, God is evil. But since God's actions are what must determine our understanding of goodness, what we are inclined to call evil must in fact be good'. We surrender our moral judgement to a God who uses His overwhelming power to bludgeon us into accepting a reversal of our moral values. Once again we may feel like Ivan Karamazov that the only proper thing to do is to reject the God who refuses to defend or explain His ways towards humanity. The tradition that argues that the problem of evil has no solution appears to have no better chance of establishing the moral qualities of the Deity than the other traditions that we have considered.

So far we have considered a number of approaches to the problem of evil and have found difficulties with them all. I have argued that the Christian presentation of God's punitive or educative purpose is unsatisfactory as a justification for the many forms of suffering around us. And it is possible to criticise the idea that no solution to the problem can be offered.

From the Buddhist religious tradition there is the sophisticated argument that suffering is neither unjust nor ultimately real. I have suggested that there are difficulties in the Buddhist approach, too, that need careful examination, although discussion of them has been limited because an attempt to consider, for instance, the nature of free will would take us into areas that would effectively make our topic unmanageable.

In the next chapter I shall attempt to outline an acceptable solution to the problem of evil. As in the consideration of God's 'natural' qualities, any attempt to describe what might be said in answer to the question, 'Why is there so much suffering in the world?' cannot possibly claim to provide 'the answer'. But perhaps some useful things can be said in order to give some form of credibility to the theist position, whether or not it is finally found to be tenable.

notes

Augustine (354-430) Eventually Bishop of Hippo in Carthage, North Africa, St Augustine is gest known for his complex pilgrimage towards Christianity. Intellectually, it took him through a number of different religious and philosophical traditions, and emotionally through a complex relationship with two women. One was his Christian mother, Monica, the other was a woman with whom he had a strong sexual relationship that eventually resolved itself into guilt and an attitude towards sex that has arguably had a profoundly unfortunate effect upon Western Christian moral teaching. Brilliant in their style and argument (he originally intended to be a lawyer), Augustine's *Confessions* and his long work on political thought, *De Civitate Dei (The City of God)*, are still foundation documents of Western Christian thinking.

Buddha (dates unknown) It is difficult to know much accurate information about the life of the Buddha, who lived at a time when there were no materials for writing in India, and when the prevailing religious tradition was one of oral rather than written transmission of information. From Buddhist traditions we can be reasonably sure that he was a princeling born into the Gotama clan living near the border of India and present-day Nepal. After a royal upbringing he renounced his wealth and family, studied under various spiritual teachers, and had a profound religious experience

— an experience of self-realisation — under a tree in a place known as Bodh-gaya. For the rest of a long life he imparted his teaching both to close disciples and to the public at large. Unlike Jesus, he appears to have founded a community which understood and preserved his teaching before his death.

Calvin (1509-1564) The most important architect of the Protestant Reformation after Martin Luther, Calvin transformed Luther's ideas into a systematic theology that became the basis for 'Reformed' or Calvinist thinking in Christianity. His key doctrine of 'Predestination' was only the logical extension of Luther's commitment to 'justification by faith alone', to the idea that faith in God is not the product of our own human efforts, but of God's prior decision to choose some but not others as His ministers.

Irenaeus (130-200) Living only a century and a half after the death of Christ, Irenaeus was probably the first Christian theologian to write as if he belonged to a church with formal doctrines and organisation, rather than to one of several scattered, persecuted Christian communities. He eventually became Bishop of Lyons in about 180, and in some traditions died a martyr's death.

Origen (185-255) A highly original theologian who despite his severe moral rigorism (he was supposed to have castrated himself in accordance with Jesus' command that his followers become 'Eunuchs for the Kingdom of God') had a widely roving and thoughtful mind which often led him to clash with the ecclesiastical authorities.

further reading

Two books are eminently readable as an introduction to the problem of evil. John Bowker's *Problems of Suffering in the Religions of the World* provides an excellent introduction to the way in which various traditions (including Marxism) have approached the problem, whilst John Hick's *Evil and the God of Love* provides a fascinating account of Christian approaches to the issue, and offers an interesting conclusion.

6: the importance of this world

religion as 'life-affirming'

The last chapter examined several different approaches to the problem of evil. This one attempts to assess them more closely. It draws out some general characteristics of a 'theodicy' (a word that literally means 'God's judgements', but which is used by theologians to refer to an explanation of those judgements where they are most inscrutable, namely in the face of evil).

One characteristic, which we find perhaps more in the Near Eastern religions than in both Buddhism, and what is to some extent its parent religion, Hinduism, is an uncompromising willingness to give ultimate value to experience in this world. Certainly the theologians also talk of judgement after death, but the judgement is entirely based upon what happens on earth. The only thing to be taken into account is behaviour during this one life. There is no preceding chain of existence stretching back into previous lives, but only the one experienced here and now.

Buddhism has the advantage that it offers an explanation of the pain and injustice of suffering, but it might be suggested that it is an explanation that devalues present experience. The belief in samsara in Buddhism, the round of rebirth into other forms of existence, is hardly the process of enlightening education that Origen attempts to describe. It is more a wheel from which the individual needs to escape than a process by which he or she comes to maturity. The Buddhist idea of nirvana appears as a concept of release from this round of rebirth into something that overcomes it. Thus whilst Buddhism is falsely accused of being a 'selfish' religion, it could be argued that by refusing to give ordinary human experience and conditions an ultimate significance, it is bound to undermine attempts to satisfy them, including attempts that involve social and political reforms. If we can somehow escape suffering, then the edge to our attempts to end it is inevitably taken away.

There is a danger in the idea that suffering can not only be explained, but can also be overcome by a process of personal enlightenment. This view the Near Eastern religions have tended to deny. Of course, there have been those who have claimed that their experience of God has lifted them out of any sense of pain and suffering. There is much in the mystical traditions of Christianity, for instance, to suggest a complete relief from pain and suffering through experience of God. But such writings have to be set against the insistence of the mainstream of that religion that suffering may have to be endured, but it cannot be negated. Take the case of Jesus of Nazareth. The records which we have describe someone who goes to his death protesting 'My God! My God! Why have You forsaken me?' The sweat pours down His forehead as he awaits arrest in the Garden of Gethsemane and anticipates asphyxiation on the cross. Jesus crucified no more appears to have detached himself from sensual pain, than Jesus wining and dining with his disciples and earning the tag of 'wine-bibber' from the Pharisees seems to have detached himself from sensual pleasure. He was flesh and blood, and believed that life could only be experienced for good or ill through that flesh and blood. Nor are his followers offered any kind of release from suffering (although they may be promised rewards after death). The cross which they are to take up will earn them persecution and a hounding from the authorities. They may have to suffer to the end. There is no suggestion that any form of discipline on earth will enable them to become detached from that suffering here and now.

Jesus of Nazareth preached a harsh and uncompromising message about the significance of choices in this life for the next. In doing so, He certainly provided Christianity with a very crude basis for understanding divine justice. But He also provided it with a commitment to the ultimate significance of actions and attitudes taken in this world. The danger with some approaches to suffering is that they are less explanations of the problem of evil than a way of explaining it away. If life provides evidence of supreme injustice, then we are told that what we see of life here and now is not 'all' of life. There have been past experiences on the wheel of existence, even if it is unclear that these experiences are actually 'ours'. At the same time we appear to be told that although suffering is real and every practical step must be taken to end it, nevertheless, there is the possibility of attaining a higher form of existence within which we become impervious to it.

I suggest that any approach to the problem of evil must recognise the importance of this world. In this sense, I am deeply unsure about a view by many who have studied world religions. It is often said, for instance, that Buddhism is a more life-affirming religion than Christianity because it does not interest itself in, or even denies, the existence of God. (It has been said by some of the most renowned critics of religion in general, and of Christianity in particular: for instance by Nietzsche, who had a certain admiration for Buddhism whilst his view of Christianity is well-known for its unqualified contempt.) My view, on the other hand, would be that Buddhism could be seen in one respect as a *less* life-affirming religion, for it attempts to set present experience in a context that effectively undermines it. It presents that experience as determined by events outside its control in the past, and its understanding of nirvana effectively takes ultimate significance away from present experience and places it in a state of enlightenment that transcends it. Buddhism effectively waters down this life with what is supposedly before and 'above' it, whereas the Near Eastern theistic religions, committed to the view that God created, manages and will finally judge this world, may have less difficulty in according to it an ultimate significance.

The strength of Near Eastern traditions, although there have been many life-denying strains within them, lies in their commitment to this world, with all the problems that this commitment brings to the attempt to solve the problem of evil. To return for a moment to the classic of Judaeo-Christian sacred literature examined in the last chapter. The Book of Job may be a clear example of a 'cop-out' where the problem of evil is concerned, but its strength lies in its hymn of praise to creation; it is clearly in love with this world. In the service of this love, it is prepared to face any kind of moral dilemma. God asks Job whether he could make the hawks soar, the eagles mount up or the lions hunt (Job 38-9). It is shaky moral ground, since these are all carnivorous predators that were created to live by inflicting suffering on other animals: better ground might have been found by citing the elephant's trunk or the giraffe's neck than the crocodile's jaws as an example of divine handiwork! But the author of Job is prepared to pit the reality of life in all its rawness, the God who challenged William Blake by making the tiger as well as the lamb, against any moral argument that might as a consequence come the way of its Creator.

I know that this does not provide a solution to the problem of evil. But what I have sought to offer as the particular strength of certain religious traditions, their this-worldly commitment, deserves some recognition. It might be argued (although perhaps to do so would imply a rather distasteful game of moral one-up-manship) that Near Eastern religions have a better basis than the Far Eastern religions for seeking practical social and political reform because of this commitment. On the other hand, no-one viewing the nature of that commitment, for instance, in attempts to mould Christian or Islamic states, could be easily convinced that the social and political reform is necessarily beneficial.

What certainly can be pointed out is the benefit that can be reaped by all religions, if they refuse to bypass the problem of evil in terms of a wider perspective than our present experience offers us. They should never let go of the absolute significance that this life on earth has for our individual destinies. Their very prepared-ness to accept the reality and injustice of suffering at face value will help them to develop a determination that it should be eliminated. Their sense of a moral dilemma posed by the existence of evil, helps to encourage a strong sense that human beings must act to remove it. Of course, they may contain many aberrant traditions that do not provide such encouragement. But awareness of the way in which evil *is* an insoluble problem for those who believe in the goodness of God, will make them work to eliminate what they know to be a profound challenge to their religious beliefs. Precisely because they are not able to deny either the injustice or the reality of suffering, they will be committed to its removal. On the other hand, traditions that believe they can arrive at some perspective from which suffering can either be seen as deserved, or as something from which the individual can learn to be detached, do not arguably have the incentive, possessed by those traditions which sense it as a scandal to their faith, to remove it — despite the obvious truth that many individuals within those other traditions have been deeply committed to its elimination. A religion with a love of life and a deep sense of the contradictions inherent in any belief in the goodness of God, when there is so much suffering in the world, knows that nothing can be more important than to work ceaselessly to remove any impediment to glorying in the Creation that Job believed had been revealed to him as ultimately good.

the suffering of God

So far our discussion has implied that God is detached from human suffering. Where the theistic religions are concerned, we have concentrated on the question of why God allows such suffering. Is He punishing us? Is He educating us? Can we have any idea at all of why He does it? The presumption implicit in those questions is that He is external to the evil around Him.

It will be useful to recall here an earlier theme in this book. I sought to challenge in several ways the idea that God was an object separate from, traditionally 'above', the world — as suggested by the image of the old man on a cloud. Seeking wide support from the major religious traditions of the world, I emphasised the double-sided representation of God as transcendent and immanent (present) in the created order. The religions that stressed the transcendence (otherness) of God to the world were found also to stress His presence within it; whilst on the other hand the religions which were associated with an idea of God (or gods) as spiritual beings that were almost part of the world's furniture, were found also to be saying that these gods were manifestations of an ultimate reality that stood 'behind' the world as its ground. God, in the words of the famous German theologian Dietrich Bonhoeffer, was 'the beyond in our midst'.

Within the Judaeo-Christian tradition, I suggested, there has been a tendency to present God instead as 'the beyond outside us'. It is a tendency which has a specific designation, namely 'deism'. A number of classic images of God in the West have supported this idea, not least those emerging from attempts to explore what it means to call God 'Creator'. Take the famous notion of God as a watchmaker. The eighteenth-century writer William Paley tried to suggest that the world displayed every evidence of having been designed by some power outside it. He drew an analogy to someone who stumbled over a watch whilst out walking. That person would be bound to ask: Who made this? It would never be supposed that the watch had simply developed naturally, like trees or plants. It was clearly an artifice. It must have a maker. To Paley, the world as a whole was like such a watch, and gave to those who observed it a similar conviction of a divine Creator.

Paley's analogy is open to numerous criticisms. But what I want to emphasise here is the presumption *behind* the analogy, namely that God remains detached from the world He has made. Once the watchmaker has completed the watch, there is no more to be done with it. Perhaps it might need an occasional repair, and some theists have tried to understand miracles in this light (although with great difficulty, since it would seem to suggest that the divine watchmaker was unable to create something without faults). But it nevertheless exists as a self-sufficient object separate from its divine artificer, who might indeed have no further interest in it.

Arguably one of the main problems with theism is its tendency to adopt such metaphors of detachment between Creator and creation, perhaps because of the ease with which they can be understood in using simple mechanical analogies. God 'makes' the world as the craftsman 'makes' the sculpture, painting or (in Paley's case) timepiece. He then stands back from the finished object and contemplates it from afar. He looks down on his handiwork, as God looks down on the world — an image examined earlier. He may take much pride in it. Perhaps he occasionally interferes with it to rectify its faults (as in miracles). He would be sorry to lose it. But beyond that he has no further involvement with it.

It is this idea of God that needs to be challenged. It has already been pointed out that the doctrine of God's omnipresence appears to contradict notions of God as Creator (which implied that He stood outside and detached from the world as His finished product). For instance, take the double-sided character of Judaeo-Christian thinking: God is transcendent (other to) the world, but this transcendence is the form of His presence in the world. To use a crude spatial metaphor, the boundaries of God do not end where the boundaries of the universe begin. It is a major failing of analogies between God and a craftsperson that they tend to imply this, whereas the doctrine of Creation which in Christianity is 'out of nothing' (ex nihilo) suggests a different picture. It is pointing out that there is nothing 'outside' God upon which He works to mould a world, as the sculptor works on stone or the painter upon canvas. What happens in the act of creation is internal to Himself. Even if creation requires Him to establish a distance between Himself and the world which is made, still the whole process that takes place occurs within a reality that remains totally interpenetrated by the divine being. God remains 'within' the world — or as some theological traditions have expressed it, the world remains 'within' God.

In this chapter we can find a parallel to the emphasis found earlier in the book upon God's presence. That parallel is the idea of God's moral commitment to the world, a commitment that extends the question under consideration from one of the suffering of humanity 'under' God to one of the suffering of God Himself. Not only is it wrong to distance God from humanity at the physical level. He is not distant from it at the moral or emotional level either.

The idea of God's suffering forces a re-evaluation of God's relation to the world. It is an idea that has been picked up in a number of theological writings written within the Judaeo-Christian tradition over the last twenty years, and as in the last chapter it is with this tradition that we conclude, although more because of our personal familiarity with it than because similar points cannot be made from the perspective of other religious traditions.

These writings have re-examined the traditional idea that God is 'impassible' (literally: unable to be affected by anything outside Himself, and therefore unable to suffer). They have suggested that for a number of reasons Christians have built up over the centuries a picture of God as largely impervious to what is going on 'beneath' Him. He cannot be associated with emotions such as anger, love, sorrow or fear, which would imply that He can be moved by what happens outside Himself. He is, after all, omnipotent and omniscient. He knows all that has happened and will happen on earth. He determines all that has happened and will happen on earth. And He cannot possibly be affected by what goes on outside Himself, an idea that challenges the notion of divine sovereignty. As a result, traditional Christian thinking has drawn from the presumption of divine sovereignty and control over creation, the conclusion that God is detached from, and unmoved by, what happens in the world.

This is the traditional picture that has come into question. What makes such questioning into more than a passing theological fad, is that it has defended its position by drawing heavily upon resources in the Judaeo-Christian Biblical tradition. It has claimed to come closer to the God of the Bible, and to have moved away from the sort of God that Christian tradition adopted in the early church period and has largely sustained until the modern day.

The God presented by the biblical writers is never unmoved by what happens on earth. He reacts to what happens with a variety of emotions:

> I will heal their faithlessness;
> I will love them freely,
> for my anger has turned from them.

> (Hosea 14:4)

Sometimes He is moved by the pleas of His creatures to change His mind:

> Then I said,
> 'O Lord God, cease, I beseech thee!
> How can Jacob stand?
> He is so small!'
> The Lord repented concerning this;
> 'This also shall not be,' said the Lord God.

> (Amos 7:5-6)

The relationship between Creator and creature is one of passionate anger and passionate love. It is parent and child:

> When Israel was a child, I loved him,
> and out of Egypt I called my son.
> The more I called them,
> the more they went from me...
> Yet it was I who taught Ephraim to walk,
> I took them up in my arms;
> but they did not know that I healed them.
> I led them with chords of compassion,
> with the bands of love,
> and I became to them as one

who eases the yoke on their jaws,
and I bent down to them and fed
them.

(Hosea 11:1-4)

It is correct to say that such descriptions cannot be taken as definitions of God. But it is still possible to draw from them a very different picture of God than the one that has dominated Christian tradition. It is possible to say that God is presented not simply in some abstract way as 'caring', but as passionately involved with the world. He is deeply affected by what happens in it.

God's 'omnipotence'

Such observations come up against the theological barrier of terms like 'omnipotence' and 'sovereignty'. God is 'in charge of' the world, it is said. He knows all that will take place in it. He cannot be presented as surprised or upset or uncertain at what takes place there. But suppose we break through these barriers. Suppose we refuse to draw any conclusions about the divine sovereignty in these terms. Suppose the will of God were to draw a fence around His own omnipotence. Suppose He knew that the very logic of creation, entailing as it did the construction of an environment within which rational beings made free choices, required Him to accept that He did not know what the future would be. Suppose that the emotion of God was the product of His own self-willed inability to know what outcome His work of creation would produce. Then He could indeed react with surprise, anger or uncertainty. He could be forced to develop new ways of seeking to realise a project which required Him to limit His own powers.

There is a mischievous attraction in traditional ideas of an all-powerful God. The omnipotent Deity of Christian tradition may be detached from creation, but there is a certain comfort in the idea that as all-powerful He will be able to do anything for us. Thus the great Christian theologian, Karl Barth, was driven to embrace the idea (against the harsh message of the New Testament) that everyone would be saved, simply because he felt that any other conclusion would undermine the power of God. It would imply that there was something He could not do. If He were unable ultimately to redeem Hitler, it would be an insult to His creative powers! By such notions Christians hide the severity of their gospel message in the warm fog of a false divine control. No wonder they approach the communion table with wormlike statements such as: 'I am not worthy to eat the crumbs from under your table'. They want to be totally impotent, and for God to be totally powerful. In that way, they lack the power to commit any ultimate evil, and God has the power to redeem any sinner. Humanity indulges in a conspiracy of surrender.

For too long the Christian tradition has obscured the biblical portrait of a God whose desperate search for humanity appears to be constantly frustrated (and occasionally satisfied) by the actions of men and women themselves. The very emotional involvement of God with creation in the biblical account, suggests an effort to struggle against a resistance that is felt as real by God Himself — despite all that might be said about His sovereignty.

Indeed, this is the biblical context within which alone we can make sense of Christianity's central doctrine, that of Incarnation, of God's 'enfleshment'. The idea of a God who 'becomes' human suggests a Deity who involves Himself directly in human life, including its limitations. It is a picture of a God who voluntarily enters a situation where, as Jesus of Nazareth, He suffers all the constraints of the human condition.

Of course, the Christian understanding of the Incarnation is itself the subject of much debate. But one interesting aspect of that debate needs constantly to be highlighted. This is the fact that traditional Christian accounts of the Incarnation — which emphasise that in Jesus of Nazareth God takes human form — involve an understanding of God's nature which Christian tradition has hardly begun to come to terms with. These accounts, with all their emphasis upon the way in which God is 'defined' through Jesus of Nazareth, cannot avoid the implication that the acceptance of weakness, uncertainty and even failure, which characterises the life and death of Christ, must be the embodiment of God's own nature. Thus, when Jesus on the way to the cross reminds his disciples of a capacity to call legions of angels to his aid but which he renounces (for instance, in Matthew 26:53), this is the expression of God's own voluntary renunciation of the sort of power which traditional forms of Christian theism insist on heaping upon

Him. The Incarnation, in its traditional presentation, is saying something about the nature of God. It is defining God in terms of a vulnerable human life. The vulnerability shown by God in the Old Testament (Hebrew Bible) as He reacts to the ways of Israel with anger, love and repentance, seeking ways in which He can draw it to Him, is precisely the same vulnerability which, as Jesus of Nazareth, He shows as a human being who will not compel others to follow Him, and in some cases cannot even persuade them.

The traditional Christian interpretations of the doctrine of the Incarnation, which talk of Jesus as 'divine', as 'God and man', provide an understanding of God which, on the whole, Christian tradition has dared not follow: whereas some more recent radical understandings of the Incarnation, that have preferred to talk of Jesus as a 'supreme human example of obedience to God', leave us with the sort of theism associated with 'deism'. In other words, they leave us with a God above and beyond the world who happens to approve of Jesus (so the radical perspective asserts) more than He approves of anyone else. What within a Christian context would be called a 'radical Christology' — a doctrine of Christ that sees him as 'merely human', although receiving particular grace from God, a sort of favourite pupil of the divine being — ends up supporting the deist picture of a God who 'looks down upon' the world from His distant throne.

The irony is that a radical Christology leads to a conservative theology (or doctrine of God). By defining Jesus as 'merely human' it offers no support to the idea of a God who is not only above, but also present in the world. Instead it tends to support the traditional idea of an impassible Deity unaffected by His creatures. Whereas what could be called a 'conservative' or 'traditional' Christology, affirming all the familiar passages from the Christian creeds such as that Jesus was 'true God and true man', has at least a powerful, suggestive and radical theology as its consequence. It raises the interesting question of what sort of God would be able to define His nature in terms of a frail, limited and even unsuccessful human being. It takes on board the sort of challenge posed in earlier chapters, concerning the nature of the divine presence.

It is not my purpose in this chapter to consider the many intricate Christological arguments through which Christians have tried to explain how God can 'become' human. But one single aspect of those arguments can be brought out. Christians all too easily find themselves talking about a God ordinarily 'outside' the world who then decides to spend a brief thirty-three year period 'inside' it, like an actor moving temporarily on and then off the stage. Whereas the Christian idea of God 'becoming' human is not pointing out a stage in God's career, the time of His earthly venture: it is attempting to state what God ultimately and eternally is. What God was in Jesus is presented as the revelation of His being, the criterion in terms of which to answer questions about the divine nature. Every Christian can recall the part of the creed where he or she says of Jesus: 'He came down from heaven', and the later part where they say, 'He ascended into heaven'. These spatial metaphors dominate Christian thinking on the Incarnation. The tendency is to think of a divine being who is 'above' us, then briefly 'comes down' to earth, and finally, after His resurrection, 'goes back up' to heaven. It is as if an ordinarily detached and safe divinity were to venture out and experience a brief moment of insecurity in human form before returning to sanctuary above.

A closer examination of Christian doctrine, however, shows that this picture is in a crucial respect misleading. The point is a complex one, involving the further complication that God is conceived of as 'Father, Son and Spirit', and that the Incarnation is strictly speaking only the 'enfleshment' of the divine Son. But Christianity also insists that no one person of the Trinity acts alone. All activities of the Trinity towards what is 'outside' it are indivisible, a famous Christian saying goes. Therefore, not only the Son, but also the Father and the Spirit, are involved in the same action. The difference is that the Son's involvement entails taking flesh (incarnation), whilst the involvement of the Father and the Spirit does not. But all three are equally involved. 'Incarnation' is a description of the Son's part in an action that is the work of all three 'persons' of the Trinity.

Now only the Son's involvement fits this image of 'coming down from' and 'going back up to' heaven. That of the Spirit does not — indeed in the doctrine of Pentecost Christians assert that the Holy Spirit remains on earth and is 'poured out' upon the disciples. And the Father's involvement reminds Christians that there is no detached Father above who remains out of the fray whilst His Son gets on with the task of redeeming humanity.

This rather esoteric discussion of Christian theology is not insignificant. It is a further way in which Christianity fundamentally refers to a God who is eternally 'exposed' to humanity, not temporarily endangered by it. The Incarnation represents for Christians the means by which God defines Himself for humanity. It is not the 'coming near' of a God who is ordinarily 'far', as it might seem to be if understood in terms of the 'descent' and 'ascent' of the Son. It is not the temporary presence of a Deity who is ordinarily absent.

In the last two sections, at the expense of some fairly complex theological argument, I have tried to offer a review of the Judaeo-Christian tradition which explores its commitment to the idea that God does not remain aloof from, but offers Himself as a vulnerable co-worker with, humanity.

A summary might be useful at this point.

First, I have set a context within what Christianity has (imperialistically) called the Old Testament, where we find a passionate love affair between God and humanity in which God is never detached from the response of the created order to His purpose.

Second, I have tried to present the Christian idea of Incarnation as a confirmation of this tradition of divine involvement. I have suggested that those Christians who think of Jesus as a human being responding more perfectly than others to God's initiative, cannot find the terms in which to express this divine involvement. But those Christians who interpret the Incarnation in terms of God's earthly presence do possess a means of expressing God's willingness to expose Himself to the vulnerability and weakness of the human condition. At the cost of some abstruseness, I have insisted that the Incarnation represents not a temporary presence of God on earth, but rather the revelation of God's eternal presence and the form which it takes. To this extent, I would see the idea of Incarnation not as a way in which Christianity separates itself from its Jewish roots, but rather a way in which it remains consistent with them. The Incarnation carries the theme of divine involvement with humanity to a climax of vulnerability and self-sacrifice, which may give some content to the often sentimentally expressed Christian notion of God as love.

Third, I would summarise these sections as offering the suggestion that the Judaeo-Christian tradition presents a God who gets His hands dirty. To the question: Why do you allow suffering? He can at least reply: 'I suffer too'. He is something different from the omniscient know-alls, unconcerned tyrants, and pathetic sentimentalists that so often compete for primacy in the theological imagination. He is not like the determined scientist or educationalist seeking to carry out the perfect experiment in a laboratory. He is too involved. He is engaged upon an enterprise in which, so far as the Judaeo-Christian tradition is concerned, He is risking himself far more than these analogies convey. That this divine vulnerability has not been recognised, even within the Judaeo-Christian tradition itself, is a mark of its tendency to return to a deist idea of God's distance from the world, and to flee the complex intellectual challenge posed by the idea of a God whose presence has to be affirmed alongside His transcendence.

conclusion

In the first section of this chapter I criticised a number of 'solutions' to the problem of evil. I am not convinced that the idea of God, either as punishing or as educating humanity, could provide a complete justification of the many forms of suffering in the world. And I am concerned that attempts to place present experience of pain in a wider context that might enable us to see its justice, and even to overcome it, effectively undermines the seriousness of that experience.

I then considered the idea that there was no 'solution' to the problem of evil. The question posed by this tradition is that of whether it effectively deprives of meaning all our attempts to describe the 'moral' qualities of God. If God behaves unjustly towards us, what does it mean, nevertheless, to call Him just? There must be some basis in experience for our attributing such terms to God.

The last two sections looked in some detail at the Judaeo-Christian tradition, revealing that it portrays God not as the external cause of suffering, but as susceptible to it Himself within the world which He has made. Points made earlier in the book were recalled concerning the need to recognise the presence, as well as the transcendence, of God.

Now to what extent have we moved anywhere towards a 'solution' to the problem? Of course, the argument of the last section, that God suffers too, is not a solution. From a cynical perspective, it merely turns the divine sadist into a divine masochist. What answer, then, can be offered?

This chapter has tried to set the argument within the context of a principle that recognises the ultimate importance of this life, whatever difficulties that causes in terms of the loose ends and injustices which this life brings. That fits in with an emphasis upon the divine presence in the Judaeo-Christian tradition, the biblical portrait of a God involving Himself to the point of self-compromise in a love affair with humanity.

The ideas of God as 'just', 'wise' and so on, do not arise from a generalised perception of how present experience fits into an overall pattern which can be labelled 'God's plan for the world'. Indeed it is arguable that God limits Himself to the extent of being unable to work in such a detached way. These ideas arise from a belief about how God has specifically involved Himself with humanity. Since for Christians God's involvement is seen in terms of the figure of Christ, assessment of the moral character of Christ inevitably provides the focus for their understanding of God's nature. That God is 'wise', 'loving', 'good' or 'just', stems from their judgement that God's presence in Christ demonstrates these qualities in a concrete way.

Of course, this raises the obvious further question: Why should anyone wish to identify the goodness of Christ with the goodness of God? Certainly they can offer a picture of God's vulnerability which may possess a certain appeal. He stoops to conquer. But this is only a theological tradition. Does it really have much purchase upon the reality of life and the pain and suffering which it brings in its wake?

What I have tried to argue is that the old adage that God cannot be both all-powerful and good, needs to look very carefully at what it means by the divine 'omnipotence'.

If the Deity is an all-knowing, all-controlling and all-determining sovereign being, then He must be able to forestall any evil. He must be able to intervene whenever pain is about to be caused, or (in an image of the philosopher David Hume) He must be able to provide a minor alteration to the brain of every Caligula and turn him into a Trajan. The picture of God as sitting above the world organising human life, much as an air traffic controller sits organising aircraft, inevitably raises the question: Why doesn't He organise them better? Is He evil or is He impotent?

But can we conceive of any way in which the logic of creation might require God to surrender His power for the sake of humanity? Such a voluntary act of self-limitation is not often taken seriously, but perhaps there are ways in which it can be given some credibility, for instance through the discussion of the Incarnation which I have tried to pursue. It could be argued that the Incarnation demonstrates that God is weak, vulnerable, exposed, and even pushed around by humanity. It demonstrates that this is true, not temporarily, not for thirty-three years until He can return to the controls and start to rule with an iron fist again, but eternally. The significance of the doctrine of Incarnation within Christianity could be interpreted to mean that what God does in Jesus is to manifest His eternal and unchanging nature as vulnerable and limited (by His own will) in what He can do.

For this reason, it could be said that the logic of creation entails that God is unable, rather than unwilling, to root out suffering. This means, for instance, that to interfere with a few miraculous adjustments to the world scene — stopping a hurricane here, stopping a cancer there — would not be like the action of removing a thorn from a lion's foot. It would be like removing the central nervous system. It would destroy the logic of the created order as such, and it is, therefore, something which in creating the world God has had to make Himself unable to do.

It may seem as though, even if it could be argued that many of the things that horrify us about the world were somehow an unavoidable part of there being a world at all, this would be no justification for creating one. We might still want, with Dostoevsky's Ivan Karamazov, to hand back our tickets. And indeed, so far as individual suffering is concerned, it is probable that most of us would want to if in considerable and chronic pain, or under torture. On the other hand, in most states of being we would not wish to say that it would be better had we never been born. In fact, human beings are very prone to preserve their experience of this 'vale of tears' for as long as possible. They at least consider it preferable to nothing at all!

We may, like Ivan Karamazov, be concerned to point to instances of the suffering of others which we find it intolerable that a good God should permit. I have tried to argue that within the logic of creation God may have no alternative *but* to permit it. Creation entails, not the craftsman who can at any moment introduce improvements to his handiwork, but the acceptance of constraints that make such interference impossible. It means the acceptance of a form of divine weakness — which is precisely what the Christian doctrine of Incarnation intends to reveal. The sort of God who makes a world is the sort of God who has to become the kind of dependent being manifested in the life of Christ.

It is possible to say: 'The world should never have been made. Better that we should all never have existed'. But it is arguable that very few people say that. They don't want to be without the world at all. They think very highly of it. They might even be willing to call it 'good' and, if the work of a creator, they might be prepared to call the creator 'good' also. What upsets them, however, are certain things about the world, certain ways in which they think it ought to be better. And in order to blame a creator for its not being better, they insist upon employing the sort of images of detachment that we have criticised throughout this chapter — images of God with all the buttons at hand experimenting with the world, and exploring how it reacts when being sent in various directions.

My argument is that in creating the world God had to give up the power to be a scientist, an educationalist, a craftsman, a watchmaker. He can be called 'evil' for the act of creation — but then, as I have said, few people blame Him for that. But once that decision was made, He had to be related to that world, not as any of these aforementioned images suggest, but as one constrained by His act to be vulnerable to the world's response to Him, unable to direct it, to interfere with it. He had to be what He revealed Himself to be in Christ — weak, vulnerable, dependent. Otherwise He could not create.

We constantly lose our faith in theism because we expect God to be able to do what He cannot do. That is usually because our ideas of divine sovereignty and omnipotence are drawn, not from religious traditions themselves, but from our own human experience of the way in which power is wielded on earth. God's power is not like that. The only omnipotence that can create a world is an omnipotence of love. It is forced by the logic of its own act to be unable to move in like President Bush to clear out General Noriega from Panama or Saddam Hussein from Kuwait. It is forced to work in the way that Christ worked, without the legions, by an example that could be rejected. That is not a contradiction of God's omnipotence: it is the *nature* of God's omnipotence. If it is to create a world, it can be nothing else.

In its doctrine of Incarnation, the Christian tradition does not just assert that Jesus' goodness is the goodness of God. It asserts that Jesus' goodness is the moral nature of a God who creates.

Although God's answer to Job might appear to be no more than the blandishments of divine power against human weakness, it could, in fact, be the very opposite. It is telling powerful human beings of the divine weakness which alone makes it possible for them to enjoy their power. It points to a God who cannot be seen as the detached controller who can be brought to court to account for His mistakes, as if He had the sort of control over the world that P&O had over the management of the *Herald of Free Enterprise*. It points to a God who cannot be related to a world with the power and glory of this one, save in the form of a self-chosen weakness that makes interference impossible. It is in order to justify His inability to heal the wounds of Job, rather than in order to boast of His unwillingness to do so, that God recalls for him the marvels of creation, and Job's inability to see what was involved in making a world:

Where were you when I laid the foundation of the earth?
Tell me, if you have understanding.
Who determined its measurements — surely you know!
Or who stretched the line upon it?
On what were its bases sunk,
or who laid its cornerstone,
when the morning stars sang together,
and all the sons of God shouted for joy?

(Job 38:5-7).

further reading

Austin Farrer's *Love Almighty and Ills Unlimited* is very interesting and provocative. It develops the argument that to eradicate pain from the world would be less like removing a thorn from the lion's paw than taking away its central nervous system — a controversial view, which many may well want to think about further!

The assessment of Christianity and its 'logic of Incarnation' touched upon here, owes a great deal to my former theology teacher, Professor Donald Mackinnon. For those who would like to follow through this line of thought in Mackinnon's thinking, I would recommend the first chapter of *The Stripping of the Altars*, and a collection of his writings entitled *Borderlands of Theology and Other Essays*.

conclusion

The aim of this book, as I pointed out in the introduction, is not to provide a definitive answer but to provoke further interest and argument. Indeed, if there is anything in the view outlined in the first two chapters, uncertainty about God's existence is a divinely willed condition of human experience and growth. Moreover, the philosophical issues raised by the question of God are profound and difficult — a point that can be advanced equally strongly against the reductionism of Ayer and against the self-justifying ghettoes of circular argument occupied by theologians like Karl Barth.

Much of what this book regards as a condition of belief, such as acceptance of a world that cannot be *proved* to be the work of a divine creator, would be regarded by some believers as the position of an agnostic. I have attempted at some length to suggest that belief, whether religious or otherwise, requires a degree of intellectual *un*certainty. Religions all too easily erect totalitarian systems of belief that compel adherents to assent to propositions which they can neither properly understand, nor in any meaningful sense affirm. Religion then becomes an exercise in sterile intellectual conformity.

There is an old adage that nothing is certain except that nothing is certain. Some people find this obvious description of the human condition frightening, and run to various forms of religious (or other) fundamentalism. These attempt to relieve their psychological weakness with spurious assurances of a sure knowledge through revelation or personal experience. The intellectual problems with this direct route to knowledge of God are swept aside in terms of some generalised argument that such knowledge is based upon faith rather than reason.

These believers in turn generate in unbelievers a narrow view of what faith in a God might mean. Hopefully, the discussion of 'meaning theism' and 'meaning atheism' has shown that, in opposition to what some forms both of theism and of atheism say, there is every possibility for believer and unbeliever to talk to one another.

My discussion of the nature of God can claim at best to have illustrated some of the problems raised by trying to define what 'God' means. I am very conscious that many readers will feel scarcely prepared to move on to further reading on the subject. At least, however, some common myths about what God is like may have been challenged by what has been said. Here also I have tried to outline what many would consider to be an agnostic rather than a theist position. Humanity can know God only indirectly, I have argued, not through recognising another being 'outside' the world, but through recognising within the reality we observe (which is the *only* reality we can know) an inherent incompleteness, a need to depend. It is as if we see a pile of books in the air. They must be resting on something, but we can never look at what they rest on directly. We can only see the books, and the way they posit something 'beyond' themselves holding them up.

In the last two chapters, my argument, once again, would be viewed by many as agnostic rather than theist. 'Explanations' of evil, like 'proofs' of God's existence, are ruled out. It is not a punishment for sin; it is not a means of educating the world; nor can it, or the suffering it causes, be dismissed as 'unreal' or as something we can detach ourselves from. Concentrating upon the idea that God involves Himself with the world (I have stressed this idea in terms of the Christian doctrine of Incarnation, but it is present in other religious traditions in other forms), I have argued that God's only answer to suffering is to share in it. By sharing in it, God demonstrates that He cannot be related to humanity as the omnipotent divine being, who can so organise things in this world that the wicked are always punished and the just rewarded. A voluntary divine self-limitation is the condition of human freedom and development. To this extent, I do perhaps end up with a version of the Irenaean idea that God is 'educating' humanity by His absence and by His powerlessness.

If, in the end, this short book appears to come down on the side of theism, it is not because I believe that I can demonstrate God exists. My argument is that we live in a world that can quite consistently and reasonably be viewed in non-theistic terms. On the other hand, if there were a God, then I have argued that there is a plausible case for claiming that He would make His existence and His goodness as unclear to human beings as it patently is. There is no clear proof or self-authenticating experience through which believers can patronise unbelievers about their failure to 'know God'. On the other hand, the confusion and uncertainty in which men and women labour to make sense of religion is itself consistent with the existence of a God who can be seen to have reasons for valuing confusion and uncertainty. 'That a man's [or woman's!] reach must exceed his span, or what's a heaven for?' may seem a poor ground for believing in God, but Browning's words at least have the merit of justifying the intellectual and moral striving that is a feature of the human condition. Though many at the end of the twentieth century bemoan the loss of an 'age of faith' in which the old certainties prevailed, it may be that the 'new uncertainties' are more suited to a real age of faith.

acknowledgements

My main thanks must go to the series editor Judith Hughes, for her patient assistance towards taming this work into something reasonably organised and coherent, and for encouraging me to write after I had voluntarily given up my job as a university lecturer.

The ideas and stimulus received from eleven years of teaching are a debt that cannot be repaid. I would particularly like to thank those in the Department of Philosophy at the University of Newcastle upon Tyne who unfailingly supported me with ideas and suggestions while their own department (unlike mine in Religious Studies) was run down and finally closed by the university. Thanks must also go to the head of the Department of Religious Studies, Bernard Reardon, for his constant stimulation.

I would also like to acknowledge the influence of a teacher in Cambridge, Professor Donald Mackinnon, who always held out to me the ideal of bringing the worlds of philosophy and theology together. His influence as a theologian helped me to appreciate the importance of philosophy, and his vision of religion more than any other forms the basis of my general approach. That said, the flaws and eccentricities of this short work are entirely my own responsibility!

bibliography

Alves, Ruben, *Protestantism and Repression* (SCM 1986)

Ayer, Alfred J., *Language, Truth and Logic* (Penguin, 1972)

Bowker, John, *Problems of Suffering in the Religions of the World* (Cambridge University Press, 1970)

Buber, Martin, *I and Thou* (T. and T.Clark, 1937)

Charlesworth, M.J., *Philosophy of Religion: The Historic Approaches* (Macmillan, 1972)

Farrer, Austin, *Love Almighty and Ills Unlimited* (Collins, 1962)

Ferré, Frederick, *Language, Logic and God* (Fontana, 1970)

Flew, Antony and Macintyre, Alasdair, *New Essays in Philosophical Theology* (SCM, 1955)

Flew, Antony, *God and Philosophy* (Hutchinson, 1966)

Hebblethwaite, Brian, *The Problems of Theology* (Cambridge University Press, 1980)

Hick, John, *The Existence of God* (Macmillan, 1964)

———— *Arguments for the Existence of God* (Seabury, 1971)

———— *God and the Universe of Faiths* (Macmillan, 1973)

———— *Evil and the God of Love* (Fontana, 1968)

Hinnells, J.R. (ed.), *A Handbook of Living Religions* (Penguin, 1984)

Holm, Jean, *The Study of Religions* (Sheldon, 1977)

Jantzen, Grace, *God's World, God's Body* (Longmans, 1984)

Küng, Hans, *Does God Exist?* (Collins, 1980)

Mackinnon, Donald, *The Stripping of the Altars* (Fontana, 1969)

———————— *Borderlands of Theology and Other Essays* (Lutterworth, 1968)

Mascall, E.L., *He Who Is* (Longmans, 1943)

———— *Existence and Analogy* (Longmans, 1949)

McFague, Sallie, *Models of God* (SCM, 1987)

Mitchell, Basil (ed.), *Faith and Logic* (George Allen & Unwin, 1957)

Owen, H.P., *Christian Theism: A Study in its Basic Principles*
    (T & T Clark, 1984)
Robinson, J.A.T., *Honest to God* (SCM, 1963)
Swinburne, Richard, *The Coherence of Theism* (Clarendon
    Press, 1977)
——————————— *The Existence of God* (Clarendon Press, 1979)
——————————— *Faith and Reason* (Clarendon Press, 1981)
Towler, Robert, *The Need for Certainty* (Routledge & Kegan
    Paul, 1984)
Walsh, W.H., *Metaphysics* (Hutchinson, 1963)
Zaehner, R.C. (ed.), *The Concise Encyclopaedia of Living Faiths*
    (Hutchinson, 1971)

index